JET ANNUAL 1973

Contents

Standard Book No. 850370-01-9

65p

THE KIDS OF STALAG 41
NIPPER LONG
MUSCLES MILLER
WINSTON
JUDGE JENKINS
DINGER BELL
KOLONEL KLAUS SCHTINK WAS THE KOMMANDANT OF A PRISONER-OF-WAR CAMP, STALAG 41, DURING WORLD WAR II . . . AND IT WAS A JOB NO ONE WANTED, FOR STALAG 41 WAS FULL OF BRITISH BOYS, AND THEY GAVE SCHTINK A TERRIBLE TIME!
YOU TWO ARE DER TROUBLE-MAKERS! SO I HAF DER ARRANGEMENTS MADE TO GET RID OF YOU! YOU ARE TO BE TRANSFERRED TO ANUDDER PRISON CAMP!
HEY, WE DON'T WANT A TRANSFER!
ALL OUR PALS ARE HERE!
YEAH . . . YOU CAN'T SPLIT US UP!
SHUT YOUR STUPID BRITISH PIG-BOY FACES! GET YOUR THINGS TOGETHER . . . YOU LEAVE IN TEN MINUTES!

AND SO, WINSTON SMITH AND DINGER BELL LEFT STALAG 41 . . .
CHEERIO, WINSTON! BE GOOD!
SO LONG, DINGER! KEEP YOUR CHIN UP!
DON'T WORRY, CHAPS . . . WE'LL BE BACK!
OL' STINKY WILL BE GLAD TO GET US BACK . . . HE'LL MISS US SO MUCH!

WELL, WHERE'S THE TRANSPORT, STINKY? WE'RE READY TO GO!
TRANSPORT? VOT DO YOU THINK THIS IS? . A HOLIDAY CAMP? YOU VILL VALK TO STALAG 98 . . . WITH FAT HANS TO ESCORT YOU!
VALK TO STALAG 98! OH MEIN POOR OLD FEET! DAT IS DER ONE HUNDRED AND FIFTY MILES!

THEY SET OUT . . .
YOU'LL BE WORN OUT BY THE TIME WE GET THERE, FAT HANS! IT'S NOT FAIR. YOU SHOULD HAVE A BIKE AT LEAST!
JA, MEIN LITTLE BRITISH PIG-BOY! MEIN POOR OLD TROTTERS ARE KILLING ME ALREADY!

LEAVE IT TO US, FAT HANS! WE'LL ARRANGE TRANSPORT!
IF YOU CAN DO THAT, BRITISH PIG-BOY . . . FAT HANS VILL BE GRATEFUL TO YOU! I VILL NOT KICK YOU FOR VUN WHOLE DAY!

IN THE PHONE BOX, WINSTON DIALLED STALAG 41.
HALLO? IS DAT DER KOLONEL SCHTINK, KOMMANDANT OF STALAG 41? DIS IS WAFFEN S.S. STORMFUHRER ADOLF "HAPPY-FACE" SCHMIDT...

IN HIS OFFICE THE KOMMANDANT CAME TO HIS FEET IN ALARM...
HEIL HITLER, HERR STORMFUHRER SCHMIDT!
"HAPPY-FACE" SCHMIDT? THE MOST TERRIBLE MAN IN DER S.S... VUN BAD VORD FROM HIM, AND I AM IN DER SOUPS!

DER TWO BOYS YOU ARE TRANSFERRING TO STALAG 98... BE SURE DEY DON'T ESCAPE, SCHTINK. DRIVE THEM TO DER NEW CAMPS YOURSELF IN YOUR OWN CAR!
JA, MEIN STORMFUHRER! AT VUNCE! HEIL HITLER!

MINUTES LATER—
SEE, FAT HANS... I TOLD YOU STINKY WOULD COME OUT TO PICK US UP!
I DON'T KNOW HOW YOU DO IT, MEIN LITTLE MAN! BUT I AM GLAD YOU DO! HO, HO, HO!

GET ABOARD, FAT HANS! I FELT SORRY FOR YOU VALKING IN DER SNOWS... SO I CAME TO GIF YOU DER LIFTS. I LIKE TO LOOK AFTER MEIN MEN!
DANKE, HERR KOLONEL!
COR, THE FIBBING OLD DEVIL!

NOT YOU... PIG-BOYS! YOU VILL VALK! DER GERMAN MOTOR-CARS IS ONLY FOR DER GERMAN PEOPLES!
COR, MEAN OLD ROTTERS!
HO, HO, HO! VOT HARD LUCKS, AS YOU BRITISH SAY!

GRRRR! I HATE DER COLD VEATHERS, FAT HANS! I VOULD LIKE TO GIF DER BRITISH PIG-BOYS A GOOT THRASHING FOR MAKING ME COME OUT IN DIS COLDNESS!
HEY, WINSTON— GRAB A SKI-POLE!

A FEW MOMENTS LATER...
I HAF HAD ENOUGH. TELL DER PIG-BOYS TO MOVE AT DER DOUBLE, FAT HANS. DER SOONER VE CAN GET TO STALAG 98...DER SOONER VE GET OUT OF DER NASTY SNOW.
JA, HERR KOMMANDANT!
GO AS FAST AS YOU LIKE, MATE... WE'LL KEEP UP!

TWENTY MILES AN HOUR! VE VILL LEAVE DER PRISONERS BEHIND IF VE KEEP UP DIS PACE!
NEIN, MEIN KOMMANDANT... DEY ARE GOOD RUNNERS. DEY ARE CLOSE AT DER BACKS!
GO FASTER IF YOU LIKE...WE CAN TAKE IT!

FORTY MILES AN HOUR! DEY CANNOT RUN THAT FAST, FAT HANS!
WRONG, HERR KOLONEL... DER BOYS ARE STILL CLOSE BEHIND!

WE'RE STILL HERE!
FASTER! THIS IS GREAT, STINKY!
FASTER, DEY SAY? MEIN GOOTNESS, VOT FANTASTICAL RUNNERS DEY ARE!

DIS IS MADNESS! VE DRIVE AT DER EIGHTY MILES AN HOUR! DESE PIG-BOYS ARE RUNNING FASTER DAN DER OLYMPIC GAMES VINNERS! MEIN GOOTNESS... IF DEY RUN AVAY... I VILL NEFFER CATCH DEM!

BUT, AT LAST...
AHHH, STALAG 98! SOON VE ARE RID OF DER TROUBLE-MAKING BOYS!
98
PAINT STORE
I DON'T LIKE THE LOOK OF THIS PLACE MUCH, DINGER!

BUT AT THE BOTTOM OF THE HILL...
OW! THE BLOOMING SKI-POLE'S BUSTED!
DUCK, YOU NUT! WE'RE GOING TO HIT THAT SHED!

OWWWWWW!
ARRRRRRRHHH!

HEY, I'VE GOT AN IDEA!
I'VE GOT A BUMP... ON ME NUT!

COME ALONG, YOU TWO. DER REPORT YOU MUST MAKE TO DER KOMMANDANT OF STALAG 98. TELLING HIM YOU ARE HERE!
OKAY, FAT HANS... WE'RE COMING!

WINSTON AND DINGER MADE GOOD USE OF THE PAINT...
MEIN GOOTNESS! DER DREADED RED-AND-WHITE SPOTTINESS! AN ATTACK OF DAT IS SO CATCHING!
SCRATCH!
SCRATCH!

I VILL NOT ACCEPT DEM IN STALAG 98! DEY MUST GO BACK TO STALAG 41, AND DEY MUST TRAVEL BY THEMSELVES... AND UNDER COVER! NO VUN MUST SEE DER RED-AND-WHITE SPOTTINESS!
OKAY WITH US, MATE... I CAN DRIVE.

SO... BACK TO STALAG 41! STINKY'S PLAN TO GET RID OF US ENDS IN FAILURE!
WE'LL BE BACK WITH OUR CHUMS, AGAIN!
STALAG 41 DER 150 MILES
DO NOT GO SO FAST, PIG-BOYS!
OH, MEIN POOR FEETS!
THE END

JEST A MINUTE!

BALA the BRITON

THE sun hung like a scarlet pendant in the brazen sky. No wind stirred the huge mainsail of the dragon-prowed boat, and the waters on which it lay were still, and seemed, to the bleared eyes of the men who lolled on its deck, to be made of glass.

Heat beat down upon these men—a heat so tremendous that it was as though they were in some mighty furnace of the Gods. It seared their flesh and dried them up; it was almost a tangible thing.

An old man, with long white hair and a flowing white beard, stirred by the deck-rail. He lifted an age-withered hand slowly and touched his tongue. There was no moisture on it. The old man coughed a feeble, croaking cough.

"Bala . . . Bala, son of Haral!" His voice was like the rustle of ancient parchment. "If no breeze stirs us within a day . . . we are doomed!"

The tall man who stood near, gazing grimly out over the glassy ocean, nodded slowly. Bala, son of Haral, who, with his crew of Britons, had journeyed through many strange lands and faced many strange perils in the search for his long-lost father, knew that what the Roon—a man older even than the oldest man Bala had ever known, and gifted with the secret of second sight—said was true. Yet neither he nor the wise old Roon could do anything about it.

"Aye—curse it! We've been becalmed now for twenty days . . . and there seems no end to it. The Gods have turned their backs on us, Roon. They've forgotten our very existence. We'll die here in this hell-spot, and no one'll mourn our passing—for no one'll ever know."

Wearily, he turned from the rail and looked over the deck of the ship, where sprawled his crew, listless, almost lifeless. To a man, they had battled with him against giants and devils and witch-spawned monsters that had seemed invincible. Yet Bala's men had won through.

Now, against this new menace, a menace of nature, they were powerless. The heat sapped their strength, and their minds. It even attacked their will to live, such was its overwhelming intensity.

Bala turned again and lifted his head to the brassy skies. His hand came up and clenched into a fist. His cracked lips drew back over strong white teeth in a snarl of impotent rage.

"By the Gods," he croaked, "that we should die like this! We're . . . warriors—not slinking curs! If I must die, then at least let me die . . . in battle!" His hand reached for his sword and drew it from its scabbard, despite the heat-scorched grip that burned his fingers. With a new-found strength, he thrust the sword into the air. "Gods of my fathers—where are you? At least let us die like men, curse you! With the wind on our faces, the clangour of steel on steel in our ears, the smell of blood in our nostrils—and fury in our hearts!"

But the effort was too much for him. He choked, gasped for breath—his arm fell to his side, and he reeled against the deck-rail. The world became dark, the sun seemed blotted out. He was losing consciousness. The thought flashed through his mind that he was dying.

And then . . .

"*Rain!*" The words, cracked and whispered as they were, sheared through the mist in Bala's mind. With an effort, he opened his eyes—and gasped at what he saw.

For the blood-red sun was slowly being obscured by a dark veil—as if a curtain was being drawn across it. There was now only a faint radiance to show where it had once been. The brazen sky was rapidly darkening, as clouds, springing suddenly from nowhere, scudded across it like huge black galleons.

Bala felt something on his forehead—a drop of moisture. Then another. And then another. Raindrops spattered down on his upturned face. A breeze played around his scorched cheeks, cooling them.

"The Gods!" he gasped. "The Gods have answered my plea, Roon! See—the sun dies, the rain washes down from the skies . . . the wind stirs the mainsail."

But the eyes of the Roon were clouded as he stared at Bala.

"Nay—I like it not. I feel it in my bones—there is something amiss. This is not the work of the Gods, O Bala!"

And even as the old one spoke, there was a cry of terror from one of the crew, who pointed up at the sky—a sky which was now fast turning into an impenetrable blackness. The sun had vanished completely, and the rain lashed down at the ship with an almost savage abandon. The wind howled, and rose to a scream—tugging and buffeting the men who fought to keep their balance on the now slippery deck.

And all at once it seemed to Bala that the ship itself was slipping away from them. As if they were being pulled into the shrieking air. He swung round to grasp the deck-rail—but it was not there.

With a shocked cry, he realized that he was falling into a well of blackness—falling . . . falling . . . falling . . .

The Blackstone Ring

Bala opened his eyes—and shivered! All of a sudden, his teeth clattered together, as though he had a fever. The cold seemed to have crept into his very bones.

"Aye, Bala of Briton—methinks you'll need furs in this land of eternal ice . . ."

Bala came to his feet, fighting off the dizziness that threatened to overwhelm him. He was in a large tent with a roof of animal hides. Tiny lanterns of delicately worked silver hung everywhere from thongs attached to the roof, giving the interior of the tent a soft light. Snow-white fleeces lay thickly across the floor.

Bala put out a hand to steady himself, and caught hold of a small, highly-polished table that stood on three curved legs, on the end of each of which were claws, that seemed to dig into the fleeces and the floor.

The man who faced him was tall, and looked neither young nor old—yet seemed a weird mixture of both. He wore a robe of purple, fringed with green velvet, and a curiously carved pendant of gold hung from a thong round his neck.

Bala groped for his sword—but his scabbard was empty.

"Your sword is safe, Bala," said the man. His voice had a curious quality to it—an eerie hollowness; as if he was speaking from far away.

"Who are you?" muttered Bala. "And where am I? Where is my crew?"

The man fingered his medallion. "As to who I am, it is of little importance. My name is Metricale, and I am a sorcerer of some note in my world . . ."

"Your world?" snapped Bala. "What mean you?"

Metricale smiled coldly. "You have quick wits, Bala. It was not, indeed, your Gods that saved you from the searing sun—but I! Ranging through the infinity of the cosmos, I saw your danger . . . saw instantly what kind of man you were, and what hazards you had encountered in your quest and surmounted. Thus have I brought you to a world that is as close to your world as I am to you . . . and yet so far that your mind would burst at the mere thought of it."

Bala's eyes narrowed.

"Why, wizard? Why have you saved us? It cannot be for any regard for our well-being, I'll swear."

"And you swear correctly, Briton," murmured the sorcerer, as he gazed at the other through half-closed eyes. "But I am an exile, and can call on no one to do my bidding in this world. Thus must I seek out warriors from another world, another time even, to aid me. And I need your aid, Bala! Something of mine has been stolen, and all my magic arts cannot get it back—for this thing, a blackstone ring, though it is truly mine, is protected from me once it has been stolen. That is your new quest, Bala—to seek my power-ring!"

Bala drummed his fingers on the table near him. Outside he could hear the whine of the wind, as it howled across—where? He did not even know where he was. He only knew that it was bitterly cold in this softly-lit tent—though the tall wizard seemed to feel nothing.

"And supposing I refuse, sorcerer?"

Metricale smiled, and there was no humour in that smile.

"Alas—you are ungrateful, Bala! I save you from death, and you will not grant me a small favour in return. However, I must tell you that your crew are . . how shall I put it?—in my safe-keeping. And they will remain where they are until you have brought me my blackstone ring. A fair bargain?"

Bala stared at the sorcerer. He saw that Metricale's eyes were green, but they were like chips of ice as the wizard stared back.

"Nay—but give me my sword, and tell me what I must do. For I am in a hurry to return to my own world."

An hour later, clad in thick furs to ward off the freezing cold, Bala strode out of the tent, and trudged off into the deep snow outside.

Wolf pack!

The blizzard had lasted for an hour now. Bala crouched under a rock overhang and hugged his knees to his chin.

The wind cut through him like a knife, despite his furs, and he no longer had any feeling in his toes. Six times he had had to clear the snow from in front of him, so quickly did the howling gale pile it up into thick drifts that threatened to smother him.

He had made about ten miles that day, on and on and up and up into the land of the eternal snows, and had seen no one. He had not even seen any creatures of the wild, but had heard, from afar off, the thin keening howls of a wolf pack, somewhere behind him.

Metricale had said that those who had stolen his ring lived in an ice castle, in the heart of the mountainous, snowy wastes. Bala judged that he was nearing his goal, but how he was to retrieve the ring escaped him. The sorcerer had said nothing about the thieves, nor exactly where the ring was hidden. The problem seemed insoluble.

And then the Briton tensed, as he heard, above the shrieking of the blizzard, another sound—the howling of the wolves again, but this time nearer.

He peered through the gusts of snow that drove at him. The howling was louder now, and carried an eerie quality about it—like the sound of lost souls moaning for rest.

He tugged at his sword and thrust it out in front of him, as a grey shape leapt across his field of vision. The overhang under which he crouched looked out over a snow slope, and now, through the flurries of wind-hurled snow and ice, he could see more grey shapes running towards him.

He licked his lips and narrowed his eyes against the wind's frozen blast. There were at least thirty of them—huge creatures, but lean and powerful, too.

He saw that some were pure white, and others, the greater part of the pack, were grey-coloured. But before he could think any more about this one of the nearest wolves, a grey one, sprang at him.

Bala met the leap with his sword held two-handed in front of him. With a terrible howl, the creature jerked from the blade and fell to the ground, where its blood dyed the snow a deep red.

Another came at him, and another. Bala set his back against the rock and used the sword as an axe,

Bala met the spring of the leading wolf, his sword poised for the kill!

sweeping it in front of him to meet the savage onslaught. Dead and dying wolves littered the snow, which was now red and brown and trampled.

Bala's breath came in short gasps as he inflicted red ruin on the snarling, ravening brutes. And then, for an instant, he stopped, as his eye caught that of one of the pure white wolves that was loping towards him.

It was an old wolf, not as powerful as the rest, but still a creature to be reckoned with.

But, in that second of time, Bala seemed to see the face of the Roon, superimposed over the wolf's head —and seemed to hear a voice within him say: "Slay not the white wolves, Bala—for they are your crew, transformed by the enemies of the wizard who set you your task. Run, now—and finish what you have to do. For only then will we be released from our torment . . ."

Bala the Briton shuddered. Was this another trick?

And then he saw the white wolf lunge at one of the grey ones that circled around him, and the two creatures rolled snarling in the bloody snow. And as he turned to run up the ice-field, the rest of the white wolves surged towards the grey pack with a howl that echoed across the snowy wastes.

Castle of ice

Behind him were the wolves and the blizzard. In front, an incredible structure that soared, glittering, to the frost-blue skies.

The ice castle! It stretched upwards for a thousand feet—an intricate mass of snow spires and ice turrets that glistened and glittered and gleamed in the cold sunlight.

As he neared the structure, a hollow roar came from the interior—a roar that boomed out over the valley behind, and reverberated back and forth across the nearby snow peaks.

Some instinct made Bala lunge sideways—and he was none too soon. Where before he had stood, a massive boulder crashed down and shattered into a thousand shards of flying ice.

Bala rolled desperately through the snow as another ice boulder smashed down near him. Ahead was a vast portal, near thirty feet across—and beyond, a gaping blackness. Struggling to his feet, he tugged out his sword and sprinted madly towards it, gaining the entrance just as an avalanche of ice and hard-packed snow hurtled down outside.

As his eyes grew accustomed to the gloom inside the ice castle, they widened in amazement at what they saw. He was in a vast, lofty hall, whose roof was so high it was lost in the shadows hundreds of feet above his head. The hall itself stretched away from him to be lost, like the ceiling, in the gloom.

But, near him, ice steps rose to an altar-like structure that towered fifty feet into the chilling air.

He ran towards it, sensing that this was his goal. Up and up the slippery steps he bounded until, gasping for breath, he reached the top. And there—lying on top of the altar, amidst a profusion of gems and jewels—was the blackstone ring of the wizard

The Briton had met many dangers in his life . . . but none more terrifying than the two giants made of solid ice!

Metricale.

He thrust it into an inner pocket of his furs, and turned to go back down the steps—then stopped, his eyes widened with horror.

For there, clumping towards the altar with deadly purpose in each step, were two incredible figures—two giants, at least ten feet tall, that were made entirely of ice.

Bala was trapped. Both figures barred his way to the entrance of the gloomy ice hall. His sword gripped in one hand, he jumped down the steps to meet them.

The first figure had already reached the steps and was climbing towards him. With an angry roar, it quickened its pace and swung a huge arm in a smashing blow to Bala's body.

The Briton lunged to one side—but the giant thrust out frosty fingers and caught hold of him, shaking him furiously. Bala hacked at the icy wrist with his sword—but to no avail. Only tiny chips flew away from where his blade bit into the ice.

The other arm came up, and its fingers fastened on Bala's throat. The cold was intense, almost agonizing. The giant gave a throaty, coughing roar, that set the echoes crashing through the vast hall, almost deafening the still-struggling Briton.

Bala made one last desperate effort—and kicked out at the monstrous being's chest. The giant was already on the edge of one of the steps. It tottered, roaring—then toppled backwards, still holding Bala.

The two of them hurtled down the steps, and struck the other giant. Both ice-monsters gave a terrible shriek, and hurtled onwards. They crashed into the floor below and splintered and shattered, and burst apart in an explosion of flying ice shards.

* * *

Bala opened his eyes. His body ached in every bone, and his head seemed to be on fire. He was lying on a bed of fleeces, and knew at once that somehow he had been brought back to Metricale's tent.

"That is correct, Bala!"

Bala winced as he turned his head. The sorcerer himself was watching him from the side of the tent, and near him stood the Roon and the rest of his crew.

"When the ice-giants were destroyed, your crew, who had been spirited away from me by them, were transformed back into men, and found your unconscious body in the ice castle. They it was who brought you back here."

Metricale lifted his arm, and Bala saw the blackstone ring on the third finger of his right hand.

"So your task is done," murmured the wizard. "And I shall keep to my part of the bargain." He lifted his hand again, and the blackstone on the ring seemed to turn opaque, and throb with an inner fire. "Now you may return from whence you came . . ."

Bala shut his eyes as the floor seemed to fall away from him again. He was flying . . . flying through a blackness that was slowly turning to light.

And then he felt the wind on his face, and heard the creak of the mainsail—and he knew that he was free to continue the search for his long-lost father.

PICTURE QUIZ

(You'll find the answers at the foot of this column)

1. Which animal doesn't exist ?

2. It's in Egypt. Is it a Phoenix, a Styx or a Sphinx ?

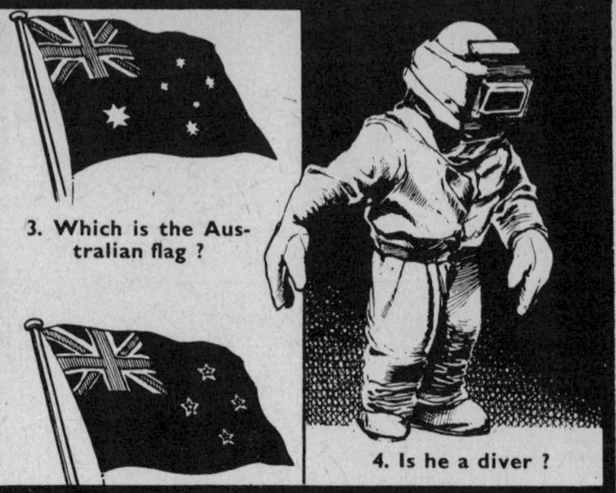

3. Which is the Australian flag ?

4. Is he a diver ?

5. There's a hole in the parachute. Does it matter ?

ANSWERS TO QUIZ

(Turn page upside down to read them.)

1. ' B ' the sabre-toothed tiger, does not now exist. 2. Sphinx. 3. The one on top is the Australian flag ; the flag below is that of New Zealand. 4. No—he's a fire-fighter. 5. No—all parachutes have a hole at the top to allow air through. This is to prevent the 'chutes from swaying too much.

Partridge's Patch
I KNOW IT'S GOOD OF GENERAL SQUIRES TO INVITE THESE SIX TOUGH CITY KIDS OVER FOR CHRISTMAS. BUT I'M WORRIED! BARNLEIGH MANOR IS STACKED WITH RARE PAINTINGS AND SUCH LIKE...
CAN YOU MATCH THE CROOK-CATCHING SKILL OF COUNTRY POLICEMAN TOM PARTRIDGE? TOM'S POWERS OF OBSERVATION AND KNOWLEDGE OF COUNTRY LIFE KEPT CRIME AT BAY FROM THE LITTLE RURAL AREA OF BARNLEIGH KNOWN TO HIS POLICEMEN COLLEAGUES AS... PARTRIDGE'S PATCH! IT WAS CHRISTMAS EVE, AND TOM AND HIS CHIEF, INSPECTOR BRINDLE, HAD DRIVEN TO NEARBY BARNLEIGH MANOR...
POLICE
THE GENERAL DOESN'T SEEM TO BE BOTHERED, INSPECTOR. AND LOOK... THAT MUST BE THE BOYS!

GENERAL SQUIRES CAME TO MEET THEM, BEAMING WITH PLEASURE...
JUST YOUTHFUL HIGH SPIRITS! DOES ME GOOD TO HAVE 'EM AROUND ... AH, THIS MUST BE THE TWO TEMPORARY SERVANTS I HIRED TO HELP OUT OVER CHRISTMAS!

THE TWO SERVANTS DIDN'T EXACTLY HIT IT OFF WITH THE KIDS. FOR, INSIDE THE HOUSE...
WHOOOOPS! SORRY..!
YOU PERISHING BRAT...! I'LL CLUMP YOUR EAR FOR THAT..!

BUT...
HOLD IT! WE WANT THEM TO PLAY WILD! IT'LL MAKE THINGS LOOK MORE CONVINCING... WHEN THE TIME COMES.
THOSE KIDS ARE RIGHT TEARAWAYS! MAYBE IF YOU STAYED AWHILE... YOUR PRESENCE HERE MIGHT CALM THEM DOWN!

OKAY, INSPECTOR! I'LL EXPLAIN TO THE GENERAL! NOT THAT I THINK HE'LL AGREE WITH YOU, MIND! HE'S SURE THERE'S NO REAL HARM IN THESE LADS... AND SO AM I!

IT WAS ONE OF THE BEST CHRISTMAS EVES THAT THE CITY BOYS— AND TOM PARTRIDGE— HAD EVER HAD...
IT'S BEEN A GRAND PARTY, ALL RIGHT! BUT I'VE GOT TO BE GOING NOW! IT'S GETTING LATE!
I'M NOBBY BROWN! I THOUGHT IT MIGHT BE DULL HERE OUT IN THE STICKS! BUT IT AIN'T AT ALL! IT'S GREAT!

WHEN TOM OPENED THE DOORS...
IT'S SNOWING! HARD, TOO! RECKON IT'LL KEEP ON ALL NIGHT!
HEY! NOW IT'S MORE LIKE CHRISTMAS THAN EVER!
YOU CAN GO AND PLAY IN IT IN THE MORNING, LADS! TIME TO GET TO BED NOW!

YEP, THE GENERAL WAS RIGHT! THESE LADS MAY HAVE COME FROM A TOUGH NEIGHBOURHOOD! BUT THERE'S NO REAL HARM IN ANY OF THEM!

IT STOPPED SNOWING SOON AFTER DAWN...AND AN HOUR LATER AN AGITATED BRINDLE PULLED UP OUTSIDE TOM'S HOUSE...
I KNEW THERE'D BE TROUBLE! THE GENERAL JUST PHONED. ONE OF HIS MOST VALUABLE PAINTINGS IS MISSING! IT MUST BE ONE OF THOSE KIDS!
B'AINT FAIR TO BLAME IT ON THEM YET, INSPECTOR! LET'S FIND OUT A BIT MORE FIRST!
POLICE

I ALWAYS WAKE EARLY! I CHECKED THAT THE BOYS WERE ALL STILL ASLEEP, AND CAME DOWNSTAIRS... AND THAT'S WHEN I SAW MY VALUABLE VAN GOGH PAINTING HAD GONE!
IT MUST HAVE BEEN THE KIDS! I HEARD SOME OF 'EM CREEPING ABOUT..!

THAT'S NOT TRUE! WE WENT TO SLEEP STRAIGHT AWAY! WE DIDN'T WAKE UP TILL THE GENERAL CAME TO...TO TELL US WHAT HAD HAPPENED!
TAKE IT EASY, NOBBY! MAYBE SOMEONE HID IT FOR A...A JOKE! LET'S ALL MAKE A SEARCH!

AFTER A LONG SEARCH OF THE HOUSE...
T'AIN'T IN HERE!
WE HAVEN'T LOOKED OUTSIDE! COME ON, GANG!

BEFORE TOM OR INSPECTOR BRINDLE COULD STOP THEM...
SPREAD OUT!
OH, NO! THERE MIGHT HAVE BEEN SOME TRACKS IN THE SNOW! NOW... THEY'VE RUINED THINGS..!
ON PURPOSE, I'LL BET, INSPECTOR! THEY PINCHED THE PICTURE LAST NIGHT RIGHT ENOUGH!

SUDDENLY...
THERE... THERE IT IS! BUT... STREWTH! IT'S ONLY THE FRAME!
IT... IT'S BEEN BURNT!

OH, NO! MY VAN GOGH... DESTROYED!
THAT PROVES IT! NO THIEF WOULD BURN IT! IT WAS SHEER... VICIOUS MISCHIEF-MAKING! THEY DID IT... WHILE WE WERE ASLEEP LAST NIGHT!

BUT TOM KNEW DIFFERENTLY...
IF IT HAD BEEN DONE LAST NIGHT THIS FRAME WOULD HAVE BEEN COVERED BY SNOW! AND— LOOK... THOSE ARE FRESH PHEASANT TRACKS! YOU CAN SEE WHERE IT WALKED AROUND IT!
THIS WAS THROWN OUT HERE EARLY THIS MORNING... AFTER THE SNOW STOPPED!

WE KNOW THE BOYS WERE ASLEEP THIS MORNING... BECAUSE YOU SAW THEM, GENERAL! SO IT WASN'T THEM!
BUT... BUT IF IT WAS A REAL THIEF WHY WOULD HE BURN THE PICTURE!

TWO REASONS, GENERAL! TO MAKE IT SEEM THE KIND OF A THING A HOOLIGAN MIGHT DO! IN OTHER WORDS, TO PUT THE BLAME ON THESE BOYS! ALSO, TO STOP THE POLICE CONTINUING TO SEARCH FOR IT..!
YOU... YOU MEAN... THEY BURNT SOME OTHER WORTHLESS PICTURE... TO PUT US OFF THE SCENT! BUT WHO... WHO WAS IT?

WELL, THERE BE ONLY TWO OTHER PEOPLE IN THE HOUSE..!
THE SERVANTS! WHAT... WHAT..? THEY'VE GONE!
THEY'VE DONE A BUNK! LISTEN!... THAT'S THEIR CAR!
VAAAROOOOOOOM!

THEY DASHED TO THE MANOR GATES...
TCHAH! THERE'S A SET OF CAR TRACKS ON BOTH ROADS! WE... WE CAN'T TELL WHICH ONE THEY'VE TAKEN!

BUT TOM PARTRIDGE KNEW AT ONCE...
THEY WENT THIS WAY! IT LEADS TO CURVE HILL! COME ON!
I'LL GET THE CAR!
CAN YOU SPOT THE CLUE?

AND...
WE DID IT! COME ON! TOM MIGHT NEED SOME MORE HELP TO CAPTURE THE VILLAINS!
AAAAAHHHHH!

BUT...ALL THE FIGHT HAD BEEN KNOCKED OUT OF THE CROOKS...
IT'S ALL RIGHT, LADS! THEY'LL COME QUIETLY! THEY'VE HAD ENOUGH!
DARN YOU, COPPER! AND DARN THOSE PERISHIN' KIDS!

LATER...
MY VAN GOGH! YOU'VE GOT IT BACK!
IT WAS IN THE BOOT OF THEIR CAR! BUT WE WOULD HAVE LOST IT... IF IT HADN'T BEEN FOR NOBBY AND HIS PALS!

AND WE WOULD HAVE BEEN BLAMED IF IT HADN'T BEEN FOR YOU, TOM! YOU SPOTTED THOSE PHEASANT TRACKS...!
THE ONLY THING THAT PUZZLES ME NOW, PARTRIDGE, IS HOW YOU KNEW WHICH ROAD THEY'D TAKEN!

SIMPLE, INSPECTOR. THE CAR ON THE OTHER ROAD KNOCKED THE SNOW OFF THE BRANCH OVERHANGING THE ROAD! BUT THEM TWO THIEVES WERE DRIVING A MINI-CAR... AND YOU CAN SEE IT PASSED RIGHT UNDER THIS BRANCH!
THE END

The GEORDIES

DURHAM LIGHT INFANTRY

THEIR STORY IS THE AGE-LONG STORY OF THE BRITISH SOLDIER'S SUPREME QUALITIES... ENDURANCE, COURAGE, CHEERFULNESS IN THE FACE OF DANGER —AS IN THE NORTH AFRICAN CAMPAIGNS OF 1940-43, WHEN THE "GEORDIES" SANG AS THEY WENT INTO BATTLE!

... GANGIN' ALANG THE SCOTSWOOD ROAD ... TO SEE THE BLAYDON RACES.

DESCENDED FROM THE 68TH REGIMENT OF THE LINE, THEY FOUGHT IN THE PENINSULAR WAR AGAINST THE FRENCH SOLDIERS OF NAPOLEON. IN 1812 AT THE BATTLE OF THE NIVELLE, THEY CAPTURED AN IMPORTANT REDOUBT...

WITHIN THE NEXT HUNDRED YEARS, THE DURHAMS SAW SERVICE IN RUSSIA, NEW ZEALAND, INDIA, PERSIA, SOUTH AFRICA. THEN CAME WORLD WAR I. AND A FULL SHARE OF BATTLE-HONOURS FOR THE REGIMENT. ON NOVEMBER 7th. 1918, THE 15th. BATTALION LAUNCHED A FIERCE BAYONET-ATTACK AT LIMONT-FONTAINE.
THE GERMAN-HELD FRENCH VILLAGE WAS TAKEN, BUT AT HEAVY COST. IRONICALLY, THE WAR ENDED ONLY FOUR DAYS LATER.
IN WORLD WAR II, THE MEN OF THE DURHAMS LIVED UP TO THE REGIMENT'S MAGNIFICENT TRADITIONS. ON JUNE 27th. 1942, IN NORTH AFRICA, PRIVATE WAKENSHAW OF THE 9th. BATTALION WAS SOLE SURVIVOR OF AN ANTI-TANK GUN'S CREW...
THOUGH HE HAD LOST HIS LEFT ARM, HE FOUGHT ON ALONE AGAINST GERMAN MOBILE ARTILLERY UNTIL AN ENEMY SHELL KILLED HIM...
IN RECOGNITION OF HIS DAUNTLESS HEROISM, ADAM WAKENSHAW WAS POSTHUMOUSLY AWARDED THE VICTORIA CROSS.
THE DURHAMS WERE PROMINENT IN THE INVASION OF SICILY. THEY DEFEATED FANATICAL DIE-HARD NAZIS OF THE NOTORIOUS HERMANN GOERING DIVISION AT THE RIVER SIMETO.
IN JUNE, 1944, DURHAM BATTALIONS WERE IN NORMANDY. BACKED BY TYPHOONS, THE 9th. BATTALION FOUGHT IT OUT WITH GERMAN TROOPS OF THE ELITE PANZER-LEHR DIVISION.
THE SECOND WORLD WAR ENDED, BUT THE DURHAMS WERE STILL DESTINED TO SEE ACTION — IN THE FAR EAST.
THE DAY HER MAJESTY THE QUEEN WAS CROWNED, THE 1st. D.L.I. WAS IN KOREA. A PATROL OF THE BATTALION COMMEMORATED THE CORONATION IN THEIR OWN SPECIAL WAY BY PEGGING-OUT AIRCRAFT RECOGNITION PANELS IN FRONT OF THE ENEMY'S LINES!
THAT'S WHAT SOME O' THE LADS FROM "B" COMPANY DID LAST NIGHT! RIGHT UNDER THE CHINKS' NOSES! COME ON, MATES, THREE ROUSIN' CHEERS...
ON MAY 17. 1958, THE REGIMENT CELEBRATED ITS 200th. ANNIVERSARY. THE CEREMONY TOOK PLACE AT BRANCEPETH CASTLE NEAR DURHAM IN THE PRESENCE OF H.R.H. PRINCESS ALEXANDRA, COLONEL-IN-CHIEF
PROUD PEACOCKS HAVE LONG STRUTTED ABOUT BRANCEPETH'S LAWNS. BUT THERE ARE OCCASIONS WHEN THEY HAVE TO GIVE PLACE TO THE PRIDE OF THE COUNTY — THE MEN OF THE DURHAM LIGHT INFANTRY!

It's A Weird World

THE crowd shouted with excitement as the two light planes flashed over the packed grandstand at a height of about one hundred feet.

"Come on, Nick!" yelled the supporters of pilot Nick Jones.

"Go, Arnie, go!" shouted the fans of rival pilot Arnold Quarton.

The scene was an air-race meeting at Frederick, Maryland, in the United States. It was September 1966.

The race was proving a close one. Quarton was in the lead, but only just. Jones was flying only a few feet away, pressing hard to overtake. Then it happened.

Jones surged forward with an extra burst of speed and, suddenly, the two planes collided! A whirling mass of metal filled the sky. Wings fell off and bits of wreckage were scattered far and wide. The planes plunged down into a field.

The spectators gasped with horror. If ever there was a fatal air crash, this was it. Nobody could survive a total smash-up like that! Ambulance men and police rushed to the mangled wreckage to pick up the pieces of the unfortunate pilots.

But, fantastically, Nick Jones and Arnold Quarton had survived—and were not seriously hurt! A miraculous escape indeed, but the world of aviation is full of weird incidents.

THEY DODGED

In September 1940, two Avro Anson training aircraft of the RAF were practising close formation flying at three thousand feet when they collided. But luckily they collided in an odd way; one crunched down squarely on top of the other, and they flew on pick-a-back fashion!

The two-man crew in the bottom plane scrambled out of the bashed-in fuselage and parachuted to safety. So did the observer in the top plane. But Leonard Fuller, the Royal Australian Air Force pilot of the top-riding Anson, remained at the controls and made an amazing discovery.

He found that his controls could operate both aircraft. So he decided to try and land both planes, locked together as they were. It was a dangerous business, but he was sure he could do it. As he flew lower and lower towards the airfield, the engines of Fuller's own plane cut out. Now things were really dicey. He had to rely entirely on the engine power of the plane below. If they stopped, the two sandwiched planes would surely plummet straight down.

Slowly and carefully, Fuller approached the airfield. Then, at a height of fifty feet, the struggling engines of the lower plane stopped dead. Fuller caught his breath, expecting the planes to drop suddenly and violently. But they didn't . . . the two Ansons, stuck together like Siamese twins, glided down to a safe landing.

Stuck together like Siamese twins, the two Ansons came in towards the landing strip . . .

DEATH BY INCHES!

Captain Hedley was probably the luckiest airman of the First World War. He was saved by a miracle in January 1918. Hedley was the observer in a lone-flying two-seater plane when it was attacked by German aircraft. In an attempt to escape, Hedley's pilot put the plane into a sudden dive at a height of fifteen thousand feet.

Hedley was thrown clear out of the open cockpit . . . and fell several thousand feet in a direct line with the diving aircraft. When the plane pulled into level flight at ten thousand feet, the pilot—Lieutenant Makepeace—found Hedley clinging grimly to the aircraft's tail section! After falling free all that way he had landed on the plane. Somehow the pilot managed to drag the lucky observer to safety.

One day in May 1915, British pilot Lieutenant Strange was engaged in an aerial duel with a German plane. When the ammunition drum of his Lewis machine gun became empty, Strange pulled away in level flight to change the drum for a fresh one. At the same time the German called it a day and flew off.

Holding the control stick between his knees, Strange reached up to release the empty drum; the gun was fixed to the top wing of his single-seat Martinsyde. But the drum was jammed. Then, in yanking hard at the stubborn drum—he lost hold of the control stick!

Next instant, the plane flipped over on its back and went into a shallow dive.

Strange's safety belt came loose under the sudden strain and he was flung out of the cockpit . . . but he was still gripping the ammunition drum on the gun. So there he was, dangling eight thousand feet in the air without a parachute, hanging on for dear life with his fingertips!

The only way he could save himself was to regain control of the runaway plane. Keeping a firm grip on the drum with one hand, he made a blind grab for a strut which he knew must be just behind his head. Then, with desperate energy, he kicked up one of his legs and hooked it into the cockpit, then the other. And working the control stick with his feet he managed to turn the Martinsyde right way up, get into the cockpit, and pull the plane into level flight.

In September 1925, the United States Naval airship *Shenandoah* flew into a heavy storm at two thousand feet. After taking a severe battering, the airship broke clean in half!

The bow section, with seven men inside, became a free balloon at the mercy of the angry storm. It was blown up and down, up and down, with the seven desperate men clinging to the metal ribs of the storm-tossed sky wreck. Miraculously they survived. For the storm blew them into quieter air ten miles away and their half of the airship landed safely.

Italian pilot Guido Caponi thought he was doomed when his little Piper Cub went out of control over the large town of Cesenatico, in July 1966. He found himself heading straight for a tall building that was under construction . . .

Caponi worked for an aerial publicity firm, and his light plane was trailing a long canvas banner which carried an advertising slogan. When he was only a moment from death, the trailing banner caught fast on a roof projection. This pulled the Piper Cub to a sudden mid-air halt, and the plane plunged down to the street below.

Then a miracle happened. A giant construction crane was swinging into position near the falling plane, and the head of the crane boom collided with the aircraft—with a happy result . . .

Guido Caponi found himself swinging gently in his plane, which was hanging from the crane's steel hook! The Piper Cub and its very lucky pilot were lowered to safety!

Strange found himself dangling 8,000 feet in the air . . . hanging from the ammunition drum of the Lewis gun of his inverted plane!

OLAF LARSEN, A MEEK AND MILD SCHOOLMASTER, HAD DISCOVERED AN ANCIENT VIKING HELMET WHICH GAVE HIM IMMENSE POWER AND THE ABILITY TO FLY. HE DECIDED TO KEEP IT A CLOSELY GUARDED SECRET...

THEN POWERFUL HANDS GRIPPED THE LOOSE ENDS...
CALM DOWN, MY FRIEND! NO NEED TO PANIC!
NOW LET'S SEE WHAT A HUMAN LINK CAN DO!
CRIKEY, YOU SHOULD'VE SAID SUPER-HUMAN! THANKS, MATE!
THE CRANE-DRIVER LOWERED THE LOAD TO THE GROUND...
IT'S DONE! I MUST TAKE OFF THE HELMET AND BECOME OLAF LARSEN AGAIN, BEFORE ANY-ONE STARTS ASKING QUESTIONS...

MOMENTS LATER, IT WAS THE FRAIL SCHOOLTEACHER WHO HEARD THE WORKMAN'S ANGRY VOICE...
I'D HAVE BEEN KILLED BUT FOR THAT VIKING! THIS COMPANY IS DELIBERATELY USIN' CHEAP EQUIPMENT AND MATERIALS!

HOLD YOUR TONGUE, BLAKE —IF YOU KNOW WHAT'S GOOD FOR YOU!
UGH!
GOOD GRACIOUS...

THAT'S THE KNOCKIN'-OFF WHISTLE. GO HOME, BLAKE... AND KEEP YOUR BLABBIN' MOUTH SHUT!

THEN OLAF LARSEN RECEIVED A TERRIBLE SHOCK...
MY BRIEFCASE WITH THE VIKING HELMET— IT'S VANISHED!

MY BRIEFCASE WITH THE VIKING HELMET IN IT! IT MUST HAVE FALLEN INTO THAT LIFT THAT'S NOW UP AT THE TOP OF THE BUILDING!

BUT ONLY THE NIGHTWATCHMAN REMAINED...
SORRY, GUV, EVERYONE'S KNOCKED OFF! CAN'T GET THAT LIFT DOWN NOW—COME BACK TOMORROW!

I DAREN'T LET ANYONE FIND THE VIKING HELMET! I'LL HAVE TO WAIT TILL IT'S DARK THEN CLIMB UP MYSELF!

IT WAS A TERRIFYING ORDEAL FOR THE FRAIL SCHOOLMASTER, AS HE CLAMBERED UP THE FACE OF THE BUILDING...

AS LARSEN CLIMBED, HE REMEMBERED SOME WORDS HE HAD OVERHEARD...
THE WORKMAN SAID THIS BUILDING WAS CONSTRUCTED WITH FAULTY MATERIALS! IF SO, IT COULD ENDANGER THE LIVES OF MANY PEOPLE!

AT LAST THE EXHAUSTED OLAF REACHED HIS GOAL...
AAH! MY CASE—THANK GOODNESS!

THE SCHOOLMASTER DONNED THE HELMET AND FELT TITANIC POWER SURGE THROUGH HIM...
NOW, WITH THE STRENGTH OF MY VIKING ANCESTORS, I SHALL PUT THIS BUILDING TO THE TEST!

IF MY SWORD CAN SMASH THE CONCRETE, I SHALL KNOW THAT THIS BUILDING ISN'T STRONG ENOUGH!

THE SHATTERING IMPACT SENT LUMPS OF CONCRETE FLYING IN ALL DIRECTIONS!
BY THUNDER, IT CRACKS BENEATH THIS BLADE! WHAT RUBBISH ARE THEY USING ON THIS SITE?

BUT DOWN BELOW, THE RASCALLY COMPANY DIRECTOR AND THE SITE FOREMAN HAD RETURNED
LOOK UP THERE MR. CARNE! IT'S THAT CONFOUNDED FLYING VIKING!

HE COULD EXPOSE OUR GAME, HACKET— PROVE WE'RE USING DUD STUFF AND POCKETING THE CASH!
NOT IF I KNOW IT!

THE PHANTOM VIKING IS COMING DOWN! THAT CRANE WILL SETTLE HIM!

FROM THE CRANE SWUNG A GREAT IRON BALL, USED FOR DEMOLISHING OLD WALLS...
JUST ANOTHER FEW YARDS, MY FRIEND, AND THEN...

THE VIKING DID NOT SEE THE DANGER UNTIL IT WAS TOO LATE...
AAARGH! I'M GOING TO FLY STRAIGHT INTO IT!

AS THE PHANTOM VIKING FLEW PAST, THE GREAT IRON BALL, USED FOR KNOCKING DOWN OLD WALLS, SWUNG STRAIGHT FOR HIM.
DON'T WORRY, GUV'NOR! THIS WRECKER WILL STOP HIS CONFOUNDED PRYING!

BUT THE VIKING'S MIGHTY HANDS REACHED FORWARD...
MAYBE MY ANCESTORS DIDN'T PLAY *CRICKET*... BUT THAT WON'T STOP ME BOWLING THOSE ROGUES OUT!

UNHITCHING THE BALL FROM THE CRANE CABLE, THE GIANT FIGURE SWOOPED DOWN...
WATCH OUT, BELOW THERE!
BY THUNDER! WHAT'S HE UP TO?

THE TWO PLOTTERS SOON FOUND OUT– AS THE IRON BALL LANDED RIGHT BETWEEN THEM, SPLASHING THEM FROM HEAD TO FOOT WITH LIQUID MUD.
UGH!
AGH!

NOW– LISTEN TO MY WARNING! YOU ARE USING FAULTY MATERIALS ON THIS BUILDING AND ENDANGERING PEOPLE'S LIVES!
TRY PROVING IT!

THE AWE-INSPIRING FIGURE LEFT... AND FIVE MINUTES LATER IT WAS THE FRAIL SCHOOLMASTER, OLAF LARSEN WHO STOOD HOLDING THE VIKING HELMET...
BUT WHAT CAN I *DO*? HOW CAN I WARN THE AUTHORITIES WITHOUT REVEALING THAT **I** AM THE PHANTOM VIKING?

NEXT DAY, IN THE CLASS ROOM, OLAF WAS LOST IN THOUGHT...
OLD LOOPY LARSEN'S DAY-DREAMING AGAIN!

HELEN YATES, THE HEAD'S SECRETARY, WHISPERED AN ANXIOUS WARNING...
PLEASE, OLAF, REMEMBER WHAT MR. GRIMSOLE SAID ABOUT KEEPING ORDER IN CLASS!
ER, YES, HELEN... I'LL DO MY BEST!

LATER THAT DAY, OLAF WALKED TO THE HEADQUARTERS OF THE CONSTRUCTION COMPANY.
I'LL TELL THEM I'VE HEARD RUMOURS THAT THEIR NEW BUILDING IS DANGEROUS... AND ASK THEM TO INVESTIGATE!

BUT OLAF WAS MET WITH A CONTEMPTUOUS REBUFF...
THE DIRECTORS ARE AT A BOARD MEETING! THEY HAVEN'T ANY TIME FOR THE LIKES OF YOU!

VERY WELL! IF THEY WON'T SEE LARSEN THE SCHOOLMASTER, THEN THE PHANTOM VIKING MUST CONVINCE THEM!

OLAF DONNED THE HELMET – AND THE PHANTOM VIKING SPED ALOFT. BUT SUDDENLY HE FELT A GUST OF WIND ON HIS FACE...
AGH! IT IS THE WARNING WRITTEN INSIDE THE HELMET - WHEN THE WIND FROM THE SOUTH DOTH BLOW... THE ANCIENT VIKING POWER SHALL GO!

INSTANTLY ALL STRENGTH EBBED FROM THE MIGHTY FRAME... AND IT WAS OLAF LARSEN WHO TOPPLED EARTHWARDS...
I'M FALLING — AAAGH!

BY SOME MIRACLE LARSEN'S HAND GRASPED A WINDOW FRAME, WHERE HE HUNG HELPLESSLY.
I - I CAN'T HOLD ON! NOTHING CAN SAVE ME!

LARSEN HAD MANAGED TO GRAB THE VIKING HELMET IN HIS FALL . . .
PHEW, THAT WAS A NEAR THING! THANK GOODNESS NO ONE SAW ME!

PULLING HIMSELF INTO THE EMPTY OFFICE, OLAF DONNED THE HELMET OF HIS ANCESTORS . . .
THE WIND FROM THE SOUTH HAS CHANGED AGAIN . . AND THE PHANTOM VIKING STILL HAS WORK TO DO!

NEXT MOMENT A MIGHTY FIGURE SOARED ALOFT . . .
THE COMPANY DIRECTORS ARE HOLDING A MEETING! THEY MUST BE WARNED THAT THEIR NEW BUILDING IS DANGEROUS!

THERE WAS A GASP OF AMAZEMENT AS THE PHANTOM VIKING FLEW IN THROUGH THE BOARD-ROOM WINDOW . . .
GREAT HEAVENS— IT'S THE PHANTOM VIKING!
THAT MAN CARNE IS SWINDLING YOU! HE'S USING CHEAP BUILDING MATERIALS AND EQUIPMENT, AND POCKETING THE MONEY HE MAKES!

CARNE LEAPT TO HIS FEET . . .
RUBBISH! HE'S LYING!
THEN COME WITH ME TO THE SITE, ALL OF YOU—AND I'LL PROVE MY ACCUSATION . . .

SOON AN EXTRAORDINARY PROCESSION WAS HEADING THROUGH THE CITY STREETS . . .
FOLLOW THAT VIKING, MURGATROYD!
CERTAINLY, SIR HENRY!

AND AT THE SITE . . .
NOW! STAND WELL CLEAR BELOW!
WHAT DOES THAT FOOL MEAN TO DO?

EVEN WITH MY MIGHTY STRENGTH I SHOULD NOT BE ABLE TO KNOCK A BUILDING DOWN, BUT IF I CAN PUSH THESE WALLS OVER, IT WILL PROVE THEY ARE DANGEROUS! HERE GOES!

THE MIGHTY NORSEMAN HURTLED FORWARD—AND THE HUGE BUILDING BEGAN TO CRACK AND FALL TO PIECES...

HUGE SLABS OF CONCRETE CRUMBLED AND FELL TO THE GROUND...
THE PHANTOM VIKING WAS RIGHT! THAT CONCRETE IS RUBBISH!
THE BUILDING COULD HAVE KILLED INNOCENT PEOPLE!

CARNE SWINDLED US ALL! GRAB HIM!
H'M, IT'S TIME I VANISHED!

FINDING A SECLUDED SPOT, THE PHANTOM VIKING TOOK OFF THE HELMET AND BECAME OLAF LARSEN ONCE AGAIN...
THE PHANTOM VIKING HAS COMPLETED ANOTHER JOB!

NEARING HIS LODGINGS, OLAF MET HELEN YATES, A SECRETARY AT THE SCHOOL IN WHICH HE TAUGHT...
OLAF, HAVE YOU HEARD ABOUT THE PHANTOM VIKING? OH, IF ONLY OTHER PEOPLE COULD BE SO BRAVE AND STRONG!
THE SECRET OF THE PHANTOM VIKING'S REAL IDENTITY REMAINED LARSEN'S OWN...
I'LL PUT THE HELMET AWAY FOR A WHILE—UNTIL INJUSTICE CALLS ONCE MORE FOR THE REAPPEARANCE OF THE PHANTOM VIKING!
THE END

Carno's Cadets

"STARBOARD, you slow-witted boomer! Starboard! Or in Cockney English, turn to the flippin' right!"

The roar of Corporal Fred Carno, Australian-born section-leader of the Redburn School Cadet Force, all but drowned the lesser roar of the outboard-motor. Its effect was to make the heavy army-type raft perform several zig-zags undescribed in the Instruction Manual.

"Yer got me flustered again!" spluttered Duffy Lewis, whose webbing belt was caught over the tiller.

"Aye," agreed Gus MacGregor, struggling to help him.

"Aye, *Corporal*!" corrected the long-suffering section-leader. "Taffy Morgan, hang on to that equipment. What ya doing?"

"Being sick, Corp!" came the miserable reply.

It was the commencement of the Cadets' holiday camp. Their destination was the small, uninhabited island of Greckmore, three-quarters of a mile off the coast. The water was shallow and tricky. The raft, of Burma campaign style, had been built by themselves.

"Remember, it's an Assault Course! Another party o' Cadets may invade us—or may already hold the island," Fred added. "Right! So what does that make us, Cobbers?"

"Ready for anything, Corporal! A state of battle awareness—on constant alert," drawled Sadra Chand, who was the son of an Indian Prince.

He stopped drawling, for at that moment they landed—by grounding violently on a sandy beach above which towered slopes deep in greenery. Everyone was thrown flat.

"Corp, I've sat on me radio!" exclaimed Mick O'Malley.

"Stone the wombats, then git off it! Beach craft safely an' unload equipment," Fred commanded. "Let's be having you! Use caution! The enemy may already be here!"

The only enemy appeared to be seagulls. They were plentiful. The Cadets' ace climber—Peerak Tensing, from Nepal—took ropes and began ascending the slope.

Pulleys were rigged to haul up the equipment. Fred, watching the operation, grinned approvingly. Despite a deal of arguing and grumbling, his small force was surprisingly efficient.

Up went rifles, cases, tent and even plump Duffy Lewis. A pulley-hook had become caught in his webbing again.

"Yer daft pudden! I'm not the perishing enemy," he hooted.

They reached the summit, took bearings and then pitched camp on a spot which held a commanding view of the island. The tent was erected. Wireless Operator O'Malley was left in charge.

"Spread out! Booby-trap the approach!" Fred Carno ordered.

His willing Cadets set about the task with glee and efficiency. The booby-traps were harmless but highly effective. Should invaders land, they'd have a hard job to take the party by surprise.

"Look, boyo! Mick's signalling—'tis a fire he's lit," yelled an excited Taffy Morgan.

Fred stood and blinked. The signal was no part of O'Malley's instructions. A bright glare rose from the spot they had left.

"Such initiative, Corporal! Frightfully good show and all that," Sadra Chand said admiringly.

"Whaaaaat? Blistering bandicoots—*the tent's afire!*" Fred Carno bellowed. "Back to base! Them other crummy Cadets may have attacked!"

They charged wildly, rifles loaded with blank ammunition. The Service tent was well and truly ablaze. More than that, O'Malley and his radio were missing. They suddenly saw Mick coming back at top speed.

It was panic stations. Who and where were the raiders? The tent was completely destroyed but they managed to rescue all equipment and stores. It looked as if the radio had gone, though! It had not returned with O'Malley.

"Where is it, O'Malley? Ya stupid great twit!" Fred Carno said.

"I left it behind, Corp! I mean, I left it here," said O'Malley. "Faith, why should I be taking it? I had my rifle! I was checking on this scarecrow I saw."

He led the way to a cluster of bushes. Perched among them was an old scarecrow. A tattered bowler was jammed on its head.

"It is indeed a most genuine scarecrow," exclaimed Peerak Tensing. "The clothes are old. It has been here for years."

Fred Carno's face was expressionless. Without a word, he pointed to where the grass was paler green than that surrounding it. The pale green section was roughly the shape of the scarecrow.

"That's where it used to lie until a little while ago. So who stood the scarecrow up again?" he asked grimly.

The eyes of his six Cadets widened. Slowly the truth started to dawn.

"Blimey, it was a decoy—a ruse to lure ol' Mick from the tent!" gasped Duffy Lewis. "Then someone set fire to the tent an' nicked our radio!"

"Too right, mate! That's the exact shape of it," Fred agreed.

It meant that the other Cadets—the 'enemy'—were hiding somewhere on the small island. Not only that—they had already successfully launched a first raid!

"Cheek! Cor, makes us look right Charlies," said Duffy.

"They've got to be found!" Fred Carno used his best parade manner. "My oath, no other section is gonna make monkeys of us. Not if I can help it!"

"Rather not!" said Sadra Chand.

The fighting blood of Carno's Cadets was well and truly aroused. Somewhere their rivals were hiding. A mock war had to be won!

A real attack!

Nothing seemed to move on the island. While guards stood watch, a meal was cooked and even more swiftly disposed of. The Cadets were hungry. They were always hungry when their fighting spirit was aroused.

"Camouflage, sports," said Fred Carno, "that's the answer!"

"Wot? *Us* get camouflaged?" inquired Duffy Lewis.

"No, they *ARE!* Mebbe they're in a cave, underground or disguised as bushes," Fred yelled.

"How do we catch them?" asked Taffy.

"By pretending to leave—and then coming back," Fred said, grinning. "Catch 'em with their Panzers down, cobber. We're not any old rubbish, you know!"

Everything was hauled up the steep slope, including fat Duffy Lewis, who had managed to get a pulley-hook caught in his equipment!

A torch beam flashed upwards, catching the Cadets in a glaring light. Next second, bullets slammed into the earth.

He'd worked it out. Destroying their tent might be a way of driving them from the island to seek shelter. Not that a night in the open would worry Carno's Cadets.

Swiftly and quietly, Fred worked out his plan. Darkness was falling when a gloomy-looking body of Cadets descended the slope, taking everything with them. A little while later the bellow of the outboard motor rang out.

"I'll steer," Fred told the former helmsman, Duffy Lewis. "It ain't that I don't trust you, mate—just that we don't want a boo-boo this time."

The raft chugged through the darkness, its note growing more distant. When Fred judged the time right, he cut the engine and handed out paddling poles.

"The current's with us! Git rowing back to the island!" he told them. "A dead quiet job! I'll wrap a rifle over anyone who makes a sound."

It was hard, sweating work. It took three hours to glide the raft to the night-shrouded island. They beached the landing-craft without even a scrape.

"Down!" Fred Carno hissed.

From the mainland, a light had flashed. It was answered by a pin-point of light flashing from the island.

"Code!" whispered the Cadets' wireless expert.

"That means Mick can't blinkin' read it," Duffy breathed.

One thing was sure—the island was inhabited. The Cadets' departure and stealthy return looked like catching the enemy off-guard.

Now the cliff-scaling started again. The lads climbed in complete darkness and there was no joking about it. A fall at night could mean injury of a serious kind.

"Good on you, fellers!" Fred whispered proudly. "Now forward on your stomachs. Keep your eyes peeled and stop if you hear the slightest sound."

They could see more easily in the dark now. Suddenly, far ahead, they heard movements. Dark figures were hurrying across one of the heights.

"I am of the opinion they definitely came out of the ground. A hideout or some such," murmured Sadra. "Oh, very clever. Positive genius, old fruit!"

"Crafty geezers! Not that we wouldn't ha' done the same," Duffy replied.

The seven inched onward. They bypassed their earlier booby-traps—which the enemy had no reason to go near—and found themselves on a section of land jutting out to sea. Far below, at the foot of a slope, water lapped against an area of beach.

"Four of them at least," said Peerak, whose senses were as sharp as an animal's.

He held up a finger. They could make him out, pointing towards something moving swiftly through the water. It left a white wake.

"Stone the perishers! A *torpedo!*" gulped Duffy.

"Yer right, cobber," Fred echoed, almost as startled. "That's funny! Wouldn't ha' thought they'd issue 'em to Cadets."

A light flashed below. They caught a fleeting glimpse of shadowy figures dragging ashore a large cylindrical object. It was heavy and was only towed with difficulty on to the beach. Taffy Morgan crawled a few inches closer. A dislodged stone rolled away, gathered speed and went spinning down into the darkness. A startled oath revealed it had been noticed below.

"Trust you, mate!" hissed Fred Carno.

"Sorry, Corporal—" Taffy's answer froze on his lips.

A heavy torch suddenly knifed its glare upwards. It flickered across a couple of faces. A short jab of flame spat.

Sprack!

Something hit the earth an inch from Taffy's head and the sting of dirt made his eyes water.

"Flipping 'eck! They're not blanks—they're usin' live ammo, Corp!" yelled Duffy.

Shouts rang from below. Two more shots whistled frighteningly close.

Fred's face set like granite. He knew enough about firearms to recognise a pistol used with a silencer. There was nothing 'mock' about the .38 ammunition.

"They're back! Get 'em!" someone yelled from below.

Corporal Fred Carno recognised both danger and challenge. These were no Cadets! It was a real enemy—*real and armed!*

"Action!" roared Redburn's section-leader delightedly. "We're under fire, cobbers! We'll show the perishers!"

Neither he nor his pals had a round of live ammunition between them. But it took more than that to worry the fighting lads of Carno's Cadets.

Rapid fire!

Men were running. They headed for the slope and prepared to claw their way up it. Again the torch blazed—and a bullet as swiftly followed its lancing beam.

"Grenades ready?" Fred asked coolly.

"Not 'arf, Corp," Duffy agreed.

"We dinna want tae waste them," said MacGregor.

The armed invaders were part way up the slope when the heavy 'thunder-flashes' were lobbed towards them. The night air detonated with ear-splitting noise.

Booooom! Baaaaaaaaam! Kerpaaaaaaaah!

Two men lost their holds and rolled, howling blue murder, to hit the sand and knock themselves breathless. The others fired wildly. A bullet whined frighteningly close to Sadra Chand's ear.

"Rifles—load!" shouted Fred Carno, voice rasping. "Shoot to kill!"

"Eh?" gulped Duffy, never swift to catch on. "We couldn't kill a blinkin' gnat. You know very well that—"

"Of course I do! Try using your loaf, sport!" Fred hissed, and flourished a heavy catapult. "Your head ain't just for keeping your two ears apart!"

Bolts clattered. Six rifles crashed out together. At the same time Fred Carno, a catapult expert, sent down one spread of heavy sling-shot.

Two men were hit. Howls of anguish rang out. One victim was quite sure he was dead.

"All in the mind, cobbers! They don't know we're only firing blanks. It's dark, see!" Fred grinned at his marksmen. "Demoralise the enemy. Make him misjudge your strength."

There was pandemonium below. Men cursed and started to run wildly for cover. A blazing magnesium flare came down next, lighting the beach as if by daylight. The schoolboy Cadets were well equipped.

"Rapid fire!" shouted the Corporal.

He reloaded his catapult and again fired as the six rifles thundered. The panicked enemy dived flat amongst rocks and emptied their own firearms in return.

Duffy hurled another flare and was so enthusiastic he almost pitched forward.

"Pin them down!" Fred commanded at the top of his voice. "Keep down yourselves," he added softly. "If the truth dawns on these coots, we're right up the creek."

His gaze was on the strange torpedo shape. What was it? It could hardly be a *real* torpedo, yet it had to be desperately important to the armed men on the island.

Fred was still thinking about it when two of the men made a run. They were joined by a third, all plunging towards the long cylinder. Their comrades from behind the rocks gave covering fire.

"Drive the perishers back!" roared Fred Carno. "Don't let 'em rescue that thing! Use the Number Threes—the special grenades!"

"You mean the smoke-bombs, Corp?" asked Duffy Lewis. "'Ere, we don't call 'em Number Threes!"

"I know we don't! But it sounds more frightening, ya daft twit," Fred answered. "We've got to scare 'em more than they're scaring us."

The smoke-bombs sailed down. They burst spectacularly, sending dense white clouds rolling across the spluttering men who were suddenly enveloped.

"Shall I use the machine-gun now, Corporal?" Peerak Tensing asked loudly.

They had no machine-gun but the enemy was not to know that!

"No! No!" spluttering yells from the enemy answered wildly.

"Give 'em one jumping-cracker," Fred Carno whispered. "Just to show the scugs we mean business."

The special jumping-crackers—War Office issue—sailed down into the thick fumes . . . .

Spak-spak-a-spak-spak! Crack-a-crack-crack!

"We surrender! We surrender!" the lurching figures shouted in terror.

"Throw down your guns!" bawled Fred Carno. "One trick from you and we'll mortar the beach!"

At that instant, another man—a guard left near the hideout—trod on the firework mines left as booby-traps. The explosions were thunderous, more smoke billowing forth.

"Enemy to the rear, Corporal. I say, how about a bayonet charge—cold steel and all that?" drawled Sadra Chand hopefully.

"No! No!" howled the rearguard attacker.

The men from the beach were hurling down pistols and raising arms frantically. They thought the fire-

The crooks were completely panic-stricken! Smoke billowed across the beach, and fireworks exploded all round them.

work mines were part of a mortar attack.

It was all over. Seven men, three of them badly shaken, were taken prisoner by the Cadet Corps. An assortment of small arms was collected by Mick 'Mallet' O'Malley. No fight was left in the disheartened enemy now.

Next day the mainland police took over. On the island was an underground workshop for the melting down of stolen gold and silver and the remounting of jewellery. The loot, proceeds from various robberies, was transported to the island by the powered and hollow device resembling a torpedo. It could be sent back again by the selfsame device.

"They thought you were kids—pardon the expression," grinned an Inspector. "They figured on forcing you off the island by burning your tent. Stealing the radio was no doubt a safety precaution—in case any message should be sent to other Cadets on the mainland."

Fred Carno saluted, lined up his Cadets and marched them smartly to where a new tent awaited them. They had already been told that a grateful Insurance Company would be providing their force with a further reward.

"'Tenshun! Don't get ideas, you boomers—no relaxing in discipline," barked Fred Carno. "That skirmish weren't nothing! When other Cadets try landing, you'll have the real thing!"

He was right! A beach landing carried out by Cadet raiders awoke the whole mainland, who thought it was a major invasion. But Fred Carno and his defenders held firm.

"Blimey, they were tough blokes," sighed Duffy Lewis, who had a black eye, afterwards. "One flippin' clobbered me wiv' a rifle butt. Those crook blokes were a real pushover in comparison."

"No training, that was the crooks' trouble," answered Fred Carno contemptuously. "Now our Cadet Force would ha' made something of 'em!"

Six panting and exhausted Cadets were only too willing to agree!

THE DWARF

PRESIDENT NIKKO OF KLOTZIA WAS ON A STATE VISIT TO BRITAIN. THE GOVERNMENT WANTED THE RIGHTS TO THE RICH DEPOSITS OF THE VALUABLE METAL, SCALPANIUM, WHICH LAY IN KLOTZIA. SUPERINTENDENT SMARMY, SCOTLAND YARD'S MOST PUBLICISED DETECTIVE, WAS PUT IN CHARGE OF SECURITY DURING THE PRESIDENT'S VISIT...
THE PRESIDENT OF KLOTZIA IS A VERY IMPORTANT MAN, SUPERINTENDENT SMARMY. IT IS VITAL THAT HE SIGNS THE AGREEMENT. YOU HAVE JUST COME FROM A SECURITY CONFERENCE. ARE YOU SATISFIED HE WILL BE UNHARMED WHILE IN LONDON?

YOU MAY BE SURE THAT THE PRESIDENT WILL BE AS SAFE HERE AS IN HIS OWN PALACE. YOU HAVE THE WORD OF SUPERINTENDENT SMARMY!

THEN...
CAN I HAVE YER AUTOGRAPH, MISTER SMARMY?
OF COURSE, SONNY!

BUT SUDDENLY...
UGH?
GLUK!
SILLY OLD SMARMY... SILLY OLD SMARMY!

HEY, COME BACK, YOU LITTLE SAVAGE!
BOYS WILL BE BOYS, SUPER. HAW, HAW!
RAGE AND MORTIFICATION SPOILED THE SUPER'S IMAGE AS HE FOUND THE LOLLY WAS STUCK WITH A POWERFUL GLUE...

YEROWWW! BY DOZE! THIS TOFFEE APPLE'S STUCK TO IT!

BURNING WITH PAIN AND SHAME, THE SUPER SCRAMBLED INTO HIS CAR...
CONFOUND THAT CHEEKY BRAT! I'LL HAVE TO GET A DOCTOR TO UNSTICK THIS LOLLY!
BUT AS THE ENRAGED SUPER SLAMMED IN THE CLUTCH...
CRIKEY, LOOKS LIKE IT'S OLD SMARMY WHO NEEDS LOOKING AFTER! HIS TYRES HAVE EXPLODED!
BANG!
HIIIIIISS..!

THE DREADFUL TRUTH HIT THE SUPERINTENDENT...
THAT WAS NO KID! IT WAS THE DWARF! AFTER HIM, MEN!
WE'LL SOON CATCH THE LITTLE BLIGHTER, SIR!

BUT THE LITTLE JOKER WAS HARD TO CATCH...
HE CAME THIS WAY. THAT WOMAN SAW HIM!
HEH, HEH, WEAR YOUR BOOTS OUT, COPPERS. I CAN WAIT!

SOME TIME LATER THE SMALL FIGURE ENTERED A BLOCK OF LUXURY FLATS...
GALLOWS COURT
ALL LONDON'S POLICE WILL BE SEEKING ME, BUT THEY'LL NEVER DREAM OF LOOKING HERE!

A LIFT TOOK THE BOY TO THE THIRD FLOOR. NOBODY KNEW THAT THE HUGE BLOCK WAS AN EMPTY SHELL, HEADQUARTERS AND WORKSHOP OF THE ASTOUNDING LITTLE CRIMINAL WHO HAD SET HIMSELF TO WAGE WAR ON SOCIETY. THE DWARF REMOVED HIS SMALL-BOY DISGUISE...
ONCE AGAIN, IT WAS A GREAT DELIGHT TO ME TO MAKE A PUBLIC FOOL OF THAT OAF, SMARMY!

BUT NOW TO SERIOUS BUSINESS! THEY'LL REGRET THEY PUT THE PRESIDENT IN SMARMY'S CARE! MY MASTER PLAN WILL SOON BE IN OPERATION!

MEANWHILE, AFTER A VISIT TO A DOCTOR, THE SORE-NOSED SUPERINTENDENT SAT IN HIS OFFICE...
IT WAS THE DWARF, ALL RIGHT! I'LL CORNER THAT SAWN-OFF LITTLE CROOK IF IT'S THE LAST THING I DO!
SUPER SMARMY STUCK IN LOLLY LAD CASE! WAS IT THE DWARF?

BESIDES BEING A MASTER OF DISGUISE, THE DWARF WAS AN INVENTIVE GENIUS...
SPLENDID! ALL IS READY! TONIGHT PRESIDENT NIKKO ATTENDS A GALA THEATRE PERFORMANCE, AND I SHALL ADD TO MY WEALTH.

THAT NIGHT, PRESIDENT NIKKO HEADED A DISTINGUISHED AUDIENCE IN THE GRANDIOSE THEATRE...
THAT'S A MOST IMPRESSIVE DECORATION, EXCELLENCY.
PRICELESS, AND LEGENDARY, MY FRIEND. IT IS THE ANCIENT ORDER OF THE GOLDEN BEAR.

SUPERINTENDENT SMARMY WAS TAKING NO CHANCES...
HE WHO HOLDS THE GOLDEN BEAR RULES MY COUNTRY!
COR THE JEWELLERY THIS AUDIENCE IS WEARING IS ENOUGH TO MAKE ANY CROOK RICH!
SPREAD OUT, CHAPS. WATCH FROM ALL THE AISLES!

THE MEMBERS OF THE ORCHESTRA WERE JUST TAKING THEIR SEATS AS SMARMY WALKED BY...
THAT LITTLE FELLER WITH THE FLUTE. HE COULD BE THE DWARF! SEARCH HIM!
SURE! THAT CRAFTY LITTLE FIEND COULD BE ANYWHERE!

BUT THE DWARF WAS NOT IN DISGUISE THAT NIGHT...
I'D LIKE TO QUESTION YOU, MY FRIEND...
HEH, HEH! THE PERFORMANCE BEGINS WITH SMARMY GIVING HIS WELL-KNOWN IMPRESSION OF A NITWIT!

HIS HAIR'S REAL ENOUGH, SUPER!
HE'S NOT WEARING ANY DWARF OUTFIT OR WEAPONS UNDER THIS SUIT, SIR.
PUT ME DOWN! THIS IS AN OUTRAGE! I'LL SUE THE POLICE!

SORRY, CHUM! JUST A SECURITY CHECK. WE CAN'T TAKE ANY CHANCES.
CONFOUNDED IDIOT! YOU COULDN'T GUARD A CHILD'S PIGGY BANK!
GET OUT OF THE ORCHESTRA PIT! THE PERFORMANCE IS ABOUT TO BEGIN!

THE CONCEITED SUPER-INTENDENT IGNORED THE INSULTS AS HE TOOK HIS SEAT, AND THE SHOW BEGAN...
THE PRESIDENT OF KLOTZIA IS EASILY AMUSED, SEBASTIAN!
HE'S JUST A SIMPLE PEASANT AT HEART, MY DEAR!

NEXT ON THE BILL WAS A MAGICIAN...
AND NOW, LADIES AND GENTLEMEN, THE MOST ASTOUNDING FEATURE OF MY ACT... THE COMPLETE DISAPPEARANCE OF THIS YOUNG LADY AFTER THE DEATH OF A THOUSAND CUTS!

THE GIRL STEPPED INTO THE CABINET, AND SOON...
EEEEK!
SUPERB! MAGNIFICENT!
SCREEECH!
HUH, THIS OLD GAG. I'VE SEEN IT A THOUSAND TIMES!

NOW... NOW WE SHALL SEE! HAS THE LADY BEEN CUT TO PIECES... OR HAS SHE DISAPPEARED INTO THIN AIR?

WHEN THE CABINET WAS OPENED...
LADIES AND GENTLEMEN... BEHOLD THE DWARF! MASTER CRIMINAL EXTRAORDINARY!
STONE ME! THAT LITTLE DEVIL'S GOT IN ON THE ACT!
BEFORE ANYBODY COULD MOVE...
YOU DID NOT KNOW THIS GALA PERFORMANCE WAS TO BE A 'BENEFIT' FOR THE DWARF!
THE DWARF BOUNDED UP TO THE PRESIDENT'S BOX...
THIS IS JUST THE BEGINNING, EXCELLENCY! THERE ARE ENOUGH JEWELS IN THIS THEATRE TO MAKE ME A WEALTHY MAN!
THE BLINDING BEAM SWUNG ACROSS THE AUDITORIUM, AND THE WHOLE AUDIENCE 'FROZE' WHERE THEY WERE...
HEH, HEH, I HAVE FIFTEEN MINUTES IN WHICH TO REAP A RICH REWARD BEFORE THE EFFECT OF MY MIND STUNNER RAY-GUN WEARS OFF!
THE DWARF SKIPPED AROUND GAILY, FILLING HIS BAG, UNTIL HE REACHED SUPERINTENDENT SMARMY...
HUM, THE OAF HAS NOTHING OF VALUE EXCEPT HIS POLICE WARRANT CARD. THAT I SHALL TAKE, AS A SOUVENIR!
THE DWARF VANISHED WITH HIS LOOT, AND WHEN SUPERINTENDENT SMARMY CAME TO LIFE, HIS MOVEMENTS SET OFF THE SMALL RECORDER...
CONFOUND IT, THE LITTLE VILLAIN'S STOLEN MY WALLET!
MY TIARA... IT'S GONE!
'THE DWARF SPEAKING: YOUR WARRANT CARD WILL BE RETURNED AS SOON AS I HAVE FINISHED WITH THE PRESIDENT OF KLOTZIA!'

EVEN SMARMY'S CONCEIT WILTED BEFORE PRESIDENT NIKKO'S ANGER...
DOLTS! IDIOTS! IN MY COUNTRY YOU WOULD BE SHOT. THE LOSS OF THE GOLDEN BEAR WILL COST YOUR COUNTRY DEARLY. THERE WILL BE NO AGREEMENT SIGNED, BUT I SHALL STAY UNTIL THE BEAR IS RECOVERED!
Y-YES, YOUR EXCELLENCY! I'LL FIND THAT TINY TRICKSTER!

SAFE AT GALLOWS COURT, THE DWARF WATCHED SMARMY GETTING A PUBLIC ROASTING...
HOW DID YOU COME TO LET THE DWARF OUTWIT YOU BEFORE A THEATRE FULL OF PEOPLE, SUPERINTENDENT?
HE...ER...CAUGHT ME ON THE HOP..THIS TIME. BUT I'LL GET HIM... WITH FULL GOVERNMENT BACKING!

THE DWARF FLICKED A SWITCH WHICH BROUGHT HIS OWN FACE ON TO A MILLION TV SETS ALL OVER THE COUNTRY!
YOU ARE A FOOL, SMARMY! I WILL SHOW THAT I AM MORE POWERFUL THAN ANY GOVERNMENT. MAKE YOUR PLANS... BUT I SHALL STRIKE AGAIN!

THE RAGING PRESIDENT'S HOTEL WAS NOW LIKE AN ARMED CAMP
STOP EVERYBODY COMING IN OR GOING OUT, WHOEVER THEY ARE AND WHATEVER THEY LOOK LIKE. THEY COULD BE THAT INFERNAL DWARF IN DISGUISE!
BUT SUPERINTENDENT SMARMY HAD OVERLOOKED THE TINY MASTER CRIMINAL'S INVENTIVE GENIUS...
HA, THE BLUNDERING SUPER HAS GUARDED EVERY EXIT AND ENTRY, EVERY NOOK AND CRANNY... BUT HE HAS FORGOTTEN THE AIR ABOVE THE HOTEL, AS I EXPECTED!
HOTEL SUPERBO

SOON PRESIDENT NIKKO AWOKE FROM AN UNEASY SLEEP, TO FRIGHTENING REALITY!
YOU?
BE QUIET, PRESIDENT, OR I SHALL BE FORCED TO SHOOT YOU, AND THAT WOULD NEVER DO!

YOU ARE, AS YOU SEE, HELD FIRMLY BY STEEL CLAMPS. BUT I WILL RELEASE ONE HAND IF YOU SIGN THIS AGREEMENT. IN RETURN YOU WILL GET THE ORDER OF THE GOLDEN BEAR, WHICH IS BEYOND PRICE TO YOU, IS IT NOT?
YES, YES. YOU FIEND! I'LL SIGN. ANYTHING... TO GET BACK THE GOLDEN BEAR!

SOON...
GOOD! YOU HAVE NOW SIGNED THE AGREEMENT ALLOTING ALL THE METALLIC ORE TO GREAT BRITAIN, AND YOU WILL NOT REVEAL HOW AND WHY... OR YOU WILL BE A LAUGHING STOCK THROUGHOUT THE WORLD!

NEXT MOMENT...
GLUG-GLUG!
DO NOT BE ALARMED, EXCELLENCY! IT IS ONLY A QUICK-SETTING ADHESIVE SOLUTION WHICH WILL SEAL YOUR LIPS WHILE I MAKE MY ESCAPE!

SOME MINUTES LATER, DOWN-STAIRS IN THE HUGE HOTEL...
JUST A MOMENT, SONNY. WHERE ARE YOU GOING, AND WHAT'S THAT YOU'VE GOT?

IT'S A SPECIAL DELIVERY FOR LORD LIMPET, IN SUITE ONE-O-NINE, SIR. VERY IMPORTANT. MUST BE DELIVERED TONIGHT.
OKAY, LAD. ON YOUR WAY. DON'T LOSE IT!

SMART LITTLE CHAP, THAT. CREDIT TO YOUR HOTEL!
YES, SIR. FUNNY THOUGH, I HAVEN'T SEEN HIM BEFORE. MUST BE NEW!

WHAT? STONE ME, I'VE DONE IT AGAIN!

NEXT DAY, BRITAIN'S FOREIGN SECRETARY RECEIVED A LARGE ENVELOPE...
GREAT SCOTT, IT'S THE AGREEMENT FOR KLOTZIA'S METAL, SIGNED BY THE PRESIDENT, AND... SENT BY THE DWARF!
AND THIS SEEMS TO BE SUPERINTENDENT SMARMY'S WARRANT CARD, MINISTER.
SECRET AND URGENT
The DWARF

BUT WHY—WHY DID THE DWARF DO THIS?

THE MINISTER'S WORDS SEEMED TO ACTIVATE A BUTTON ON THE ENVELOPE—AND A RECORDED MESSAGE BOOMED OUT...
'BECAUSE, FOREIGN SECRETARY, I WISH BRITAIN TO BE RICH AND POWERFUL, SO THAT I MAY ROB IT MORE PROFITABLY! MY COMPLIMENTS TO SUPERINTENDENT SMARMY. HEH, HEH!'
AND URGENT
The DWARF

AT HEADQUARTERS, SUPERINTENDENT SMARMY WAS ON THE CARPET...
YOUR WARRANT CARD, SUPERINTENDENT, KINDLY RETURNED BY THE DWARF! BY THUNDER, I'D RATHER HAVE HIM ON MY STAFF THAN YOU.
YOU CAN'T MEAN THAT, SIR. HE'S A VILLAIN! A TRICKY LITTLE VILLAIN! BUT I'LL CATCH HIM, NEVER FEAR!

IN HIS SECRET BASE, THE DWARF WASN'T WORRYING...
IN A BRIEF INTERVIEW, PRESIDENT NIKKO ASSURED ME HE ENJOYED HIS STAY IN LONDON, BUT NOW HE MUST HURRY BACK TO KLOTZIA TO TAKE OVER THE REINS OF GOVERNMENT AGAIN!
HO, HO! I WONDER IF HE WILL EXPLAIN WHY HE SIGNED THE AGREEMENT SO QUICKLY!

NEVER MIND... THE DWARF WINS AGAIN!
The End

Once a fairly common sight on the roads of Britain—a Foden D type steam tractor, built way back in 1927, to carry loads of bricks.

The proud owner of a Wallis and Steevens traction engine, Mr. Frank Upton, gets busy with his polish rag.

(Below) A beautifully-decorated showman's engine—used for generating electricity to drive fairground rides. A proud and weighty monster, appropriately named "Dreadnought".

GIANTS of STEAM

(Above) For all its size and weight—9 tons—this Wallis and Steevens engine raised only 4 h.p.

(Left) A 2" to the foot scale model whistles as it passes a huge 14-ton McLaren Road loco, of 1919 vintage.

(Below) Three veterans—a Foden steam wagon, a Ruston Proctor traction engine, and Fowler showman's tractor.

The Age of Steam is over. No longer do the mighty monsters clank and puff their way along road and rail . . . except on special occasions. For the romance of the Steam Age lingers on. Hundreds of enthusiasts treasure the old time giants, lavishing hours of care and attention in renovating and preserving them. More and more steam traction rallies are being held every year!

The CHERRYPICKERS
IN THE LAST WAR THE 11th HUSSARS GAINED MORE BATTLE HONOURS THAN ANY OTHER CAVALRY REGIMENT, PERHAPS BECAUSE THEY WERE THERE FROM THE START. ORIGINAL DESERT RATS, THEY WERE THE FIRST TO CROSS THE DESERT IN THEIR ROLLS ROYCE ARMOURED CARS...
BADGE OF 11th HUSSARS
TREU UND FEST
RAISED IN 1750, AS HONEYWOOD'S DRAGOONS, THE 11th HUSSARS' FAMOUS NICKNAME WAS GAINED DURING THE PENINSULAR WAR ON 15th AUGUST, 1811...
WATCH OUT, LADS! IT'S THE FROGGIES!

THE FRENCH DRAGOONS BURST INTO THE CHERRY ORCHARD WHERE THE 11th. HUSSARS WERE DISMOUNTED.
NO YOU DON'T! TAKE A BITE ON THAT LOT!
AAAAGH!

SAVAGELY THEY FOUGHT OFF THE MOUNTED ENEMY...AND WERE FOR EVER AFTERWARDS TO BE KNOWN AS THE "CHERRYPICKERS"!
THAT'S THAT! NOW...WE DESERVE SOME FRUIT!

IN 1840 PRINCE ALBERT OF SAXE-COBURG MARRIED QUEEN VICTORIA OF ENGLAND. HE BECAME THEIR COLONEL-IN-CHIEF, AND IT WAS AS "PRINCE ALBERT'S OWN" THAT THEY TOOK TO WEARING CRIMSON TROUSERS, STILL A UNIFORM DISTINCTION.

BUT THE CHERRYPICKERS' GREATEST DAY OF GLORY WAS ON 25th. OCTOBER, 1854, WHEN THEY RODE IN THE CHARGE OF THE LIGHT BRIGADE AT BALACLAVA!
THE LIGHT BRIGADE WILL ADVANCE! CHARGE!

STRAIGHT UP THE VALLEY OF DEATH THEY WENT... HEADING FOR THE RUSSIAN GUNS...
KEEP YOUR RANKS, ELEVENTH!

AAAAGH!

ONLY TWENTY-FIVE OF THE REGIMENT SURVIVED THAT TERRIBLE CHARGE...
ALL RIGHT THEN... ANSWER YOUR NAMES...

THEY STILL CELEBRATE "BALACLAVA DAY" IN THE 11th. HUSSARS, THE DAY THEY LED THE CAVALRY AGAINST THE RUSSIAN GUNS...AS IN 1945, THEY HAD THE HONOUR OF LEADING THE 7th. ARMOURED DIVISION, "THE DESERT RATS", INTO DEFEATED BERLIN...

TAFFY JONES
SERGEANTS FOUR
ALF HIGGS
JOCK McGILL
PADDY O'BOYLE

NO SECOND WORLD WAR COMBAT UNIT COULD HAVE BETTER REPRESENTED GREAT BRITAIN THAN THOSE N.C.O.S, ALF HIGGS, JOCK McGILL, TAFFY JONES AND PADDY O'BOYLE, WHO FORMED THE ACE SPECIAL COMMANDO UNIT KNOWN AS 'SERGEANTS FOUR'. BUT NOT ALL THEIR OPERATIONS WERE COMPLETELY SUCCESSFUL. FOR INSTANCE, THERE WAS ONE TIME IN WARTORN ITALY, WHEN. . .
THEY'RE ON THE RUN, LOOK YOU!
BEGORRAH! THE SQUAREHEAD SPALPEENS ARE SCARPERIN'!
HOOTS! I DIDNA THINK WE'D TAKE THE LINE AS EASY AS THIS!
I WONDER WHAT THEY'VE LEFT BEHIND IN THAT TRUCK!

ACH! A LOAD OF NAZI FLAGS! WE'LL NO' HAVE ANY USE FOR THEM!
DON'T YOU FLIPPIN' BELIEVE IT, JOCKO! NEVER CHUCK NOTHIN' AWAY, THAT'S ALF HIGGS' MOTTO!

WE'LL TAKE SOME BACK IN THAT JERRY JEEP. OLD ALFIE BOY'LL FIND A SUCKER TO FLOG 'EM TO DON'T YOU WORRY!

TWO DAYS LATER. . .
GOOD NEWS FOR YOU! THE BRIGADIER'S GIVEN YOU FIVE DAYS LEAVE. . .STARTING TODAY.
BUT WHERE CAN WE GO? THAT'S THE PROBLEM!

AN HOUR LATER THEY WERE IN THE NEAREST VILLAGE. . .
I'M SICK OF SCOFFIN' SPAGHETTI. WHAT WOULDN'T I GIVE FOR SOME REAL SHEPHERD'S PIE AND FRESH LEEKS. . . .'
OR A FINE HAGGIS. . . .!
OR SOME HOME-MADE IRISH STEW! BEGORRAH, 'TIS A PITY WE CAN'T SPEND THESE FIVE DAYS BACK IN BLIGHTY!
HANG ON HERE FOR ME MATES! ALF'S GOT AN IDEA!

WHEN, AT LAST ALF RETURNED
THIS IS LOOTENANT JOE SPATZ OF THE YANK AIR FORCE IN EXCHANGE FOR THEM NAZI FLAGS WE FOUND.. HE'S GOIN' TO FLY US TO BLIGHTY!
ROUTINE SUPPLY TRIP. TAKE OFF IN AN HOUR, FELLERS! GOTTA BE BACK HERE FIVE DAYS FROM NOW!

NOTHIN' TO IT! YOU JUST TAKE MY PALS' PLACES—AS GUNNERS. YOU GET TO LIL OLE BRITAIN... AND THEY GET FIVE DAYS DOIN' NOTHIN', WHICH SUITS THEM FINE!
WE JUST PUT ON THEIR FLYIN' JACKETS AND OFF WE GO! FIVE DAYS LEAVE HOME! NO TROUBLE, NO PROBLEMS...NO ONE'LL BE ANY THE WISER!

ARE YOU THE PILOT?
NAW, I'M NAVIGATOR. BUT YOU DON'T HAVE TO WORRY ABOUT THE SKIPPER. CAP'N ELMER HICKORY'S JEST ABOUT THE STOOPIDEST PILOT IN THE WHOLE U.S. AIR CORPS.

AND SO...
MAN THE GUNS, YOU GUYS...NOT THAT YOU'LL HAVE TO USE 'EM! NOTHIN' EVER HAPPENS ON THESE SUPPLY RUNS!

BUT THIS TIME SOMETHING DID...
KRAUTS, DOGGONE IT COMIN' RIGHT AT US!
I JEST HOPE THEM FOUR LIMEYS CAN SHOOT!

JOE SPATZ NEEDN'T HAVE WORRIED...
ACH, A BODY CANNA MISS WITH TWO GUNS TO FIRE AT ONCE!
BULLSEYE!
BRRRRRPPP!
BEAAAAAAAPP!

A SPANDAU BURST SENT LITTLE TAFFY TUMBLING...
PIIIIIOOOO!
ZING
ZIIIP
THAT CHEEKY, SAUSAGE-EATING JERRY!

INDEED TO GOODNESS! I'LL TEACH 'EM A LESSON!
THROWIN' GRENADES AT 'EM, TAFFY! BEJABERS, THAT'S NOT VERY SPORTIN' AT ALL!

CRUNCH... CRAAAASH!
BLAAAAAAMMM!
WHAT YOU WANT TO GO AND DO THAT FOR, TAFF? I WAS JUST GETTING ME EYE IN...! BLOOMIN' SELFISH THAT IS.. BAGGIN' 'EM ALL FOR YERSELF!

BUT THE HUGE LIBERATOR HAD NOT ESCAPED DAMAGE...
SKIPPER! YOU'RE GOING THE WRONG WAY!
GOLDARN IT, JOE, I'M GOIN' THE ONLY TARNATION WAY I CAN GO! THE DOGGONE RUDDERS ARE ALL JAMMED UP!

ON AND ON THEY WENT, IN A LONG SHALLOW DIVE—THEN...
YOU BONE-HEADED HILLBILLY! EVEN IF YOU COULDN'T STEER HER.. YOU COULD HAVE KEPT HER UP IN THE AIR!
COULDN'T DO THAT NEITHER, JOE! THEM KRAUTS PUNCTURED OUR FUEL TANKS. WE'RE PLUMB OUT OF GAS!

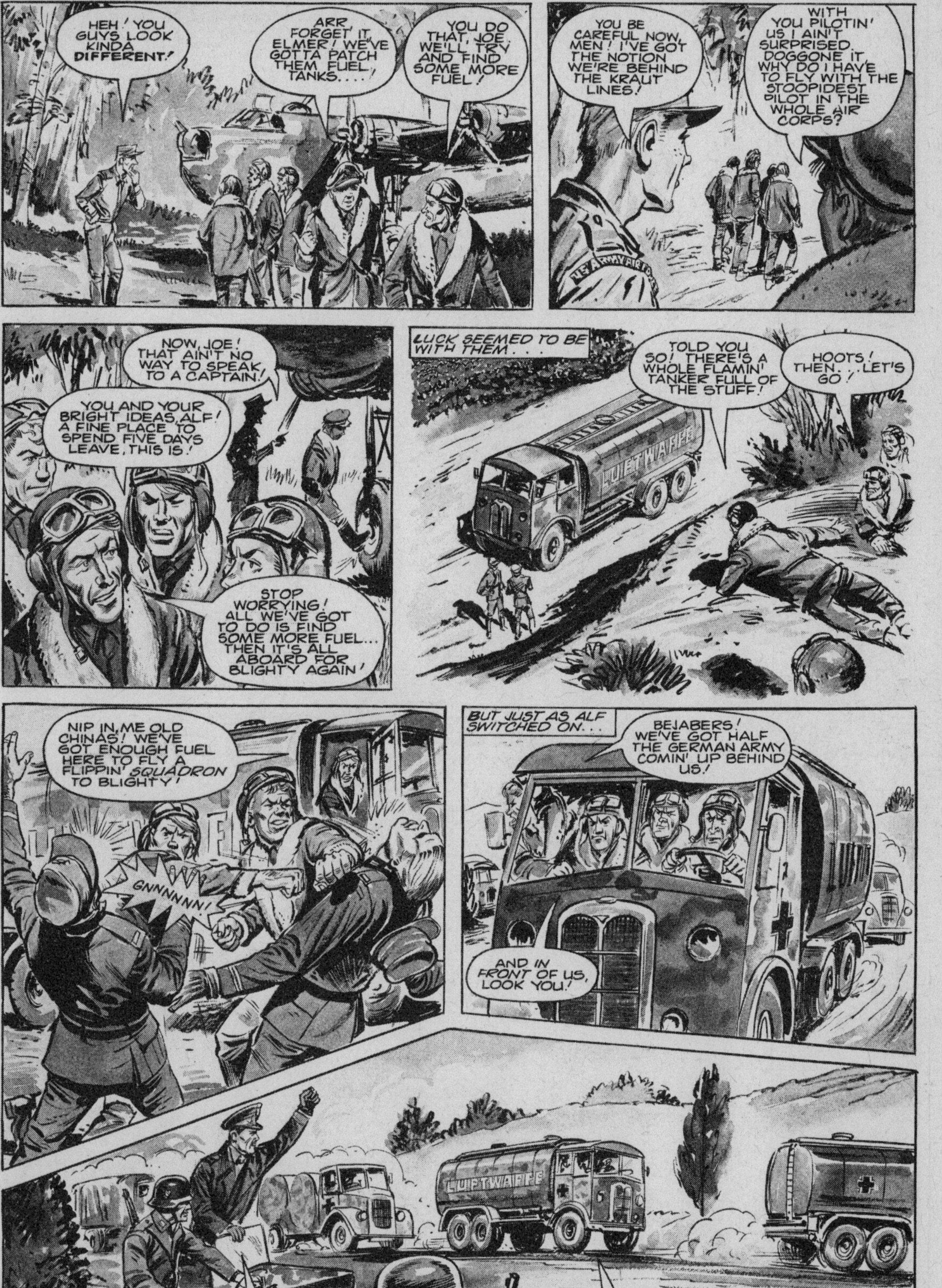

NIP IN, ME OLD CHINAS! WE'VE GOT ENOUGH FUEL HERE TO FLY A FLIPPIN' *SQUADRON* TO BLIGHTY!
GNNNNNN!

BUT JUST AS ALF SWITCHED ON...
BEJABERS! WE'VE GOT HALF THE GERMAN ARMY COMIN' UP BEHIND US!
AND IN *FRONT* OF US, LOOK YOU!

LUFTWAFFE
HURRY! HURRY! DONNER UND BLITZEN! DOES IT TAKE YOU A *YEAR* TO CHANGE A WHEEL, YOU DUMMKOPFS?
WE'RE IN THE MIDDLE OF *A JERRY CONVOY*!

WE'LL JUST HAVE TO GO ALONG WITH THEM FOR A BIT!
INDEED TO GOODNESS! BUT WHERE TO?
TEN MINUTES LATER...
STREWTH! IT'S A JERRY SECRET FACTORY!
LUFTWAFFE
I DINNA THINK WE'RE GOIN' TO STAY A SECRET MUCH LONGER
JOCK McGILL WAS RIGHT...
ACHTUNG! ACHTUNG! ENGLANDERS!
HANG ON, MATES! IT'S TIME WE WERE LEAVIN' THIS LITTLE PARTY!
STREWTH! THE PERISHERS HAVE BLOWN A TYRE!
THAT'S ME NEXT-TO-LAST GRENADE! ONLY ONE MORE LEFT!
BWAAANG!
EVERYBODY OUT!
MAY AS WELL USE UP MY LAST GRENADE!
LUFTWAFFE
THERE SHE GOES!
BLAAAAAAM!
NEXT SECOND THE BOWSER WAS LIKE A HURTLING, BLAZING TORCH.
LOOK OUT!
LUFTWAFFE
HIMMEL!

THEN...
BLAAAAAAAM!
BWOOOMPH!
IT WAS...
CLOSE THE GATES!
SORRY, MATE! BUT WE'RE LEAVIN'! WE'VE GOT THIS FEELIN' THAT WE AIN'T WELCOME HERE!
CRAAAASH!

THERE'S ANOTHER FUEL LORRY! QUICK!
BEGORRAH, LET'S HOPE THE IGNITION KEY'S STILL IN IT!

ANGRY GERMAN CRIES ROSE ABOVE THE MOUNTING ROAR OF FLAMES...
PUT YOUR FOOT DOWN, BACH!
AFTER THEM! HIMMEL, BUT THOSE ENGLANDER PIG-DOGS SHALL PAY FOR THIS!

AS THE FOUR SERGEANTS SPED AWAY...
BEGORRAH! FLYIN' FORTRESSES! I HOPE THE YANK BOMB-AIMERS DON'T THINK WE'RE JERRIES!
WITH ALL THOSE SWASTIKAS PAINTED ON THIS BLOOMIN' LORRY... THEY'RE BOUND TO! AND DROP A BOMB ON US FOR LUCK!

BUT NEXT MOMENT...
THERE GOES THE FACTORY! SKY FLIPPIN' HIGH!
BWWWOOOOPPHH!

THEY'RE TURNING ROUND! THE YANKS ARE GOIN' BACK!
THEY MUST'VE BEEN ABOUT TO FLATTEN THAT FACTORY. BUT WE DID IT FIRST!

SOON THEY WERE ALONGSIDE THE STRANDED LIBERATOR...
A FEW MORE CANS AND WE'RE AWAY!
YOU AND YOUR PAL WILL HAVE TO POUR IN THE REST! PADDY, TAFF, JOCK... GET WHAT GUNS ARE INSIDE THAT LIB! WE'LL NEED 'EM!

COR STREWTH! GIVE US A PERISHIN' CHANCE!

NOT SO FAST, YOU FLEA-BRAINED FLYBOY! THEY'RE NOT ABOARD YET!

FRANTICALLY, THE FOUR SERGEANTS GRABBED FOR HANDHOLDS . . .

KEEP HER STRAIGHT, YOU LUNKHEAD! THOSE POOR GUYS ARE HANGIN' ON BY THEIR FINGERNAILS!

BUT. . .

OH MY, GOSH!

YAAAAAAA! NO! KEEP HER... YIIIEEEEEE!

AAAAAAAHHH!

WHOOOOOOSH

ELMER! HOW YOU EVER GOT THOSE WINGS I'LL NEVER KNOW!

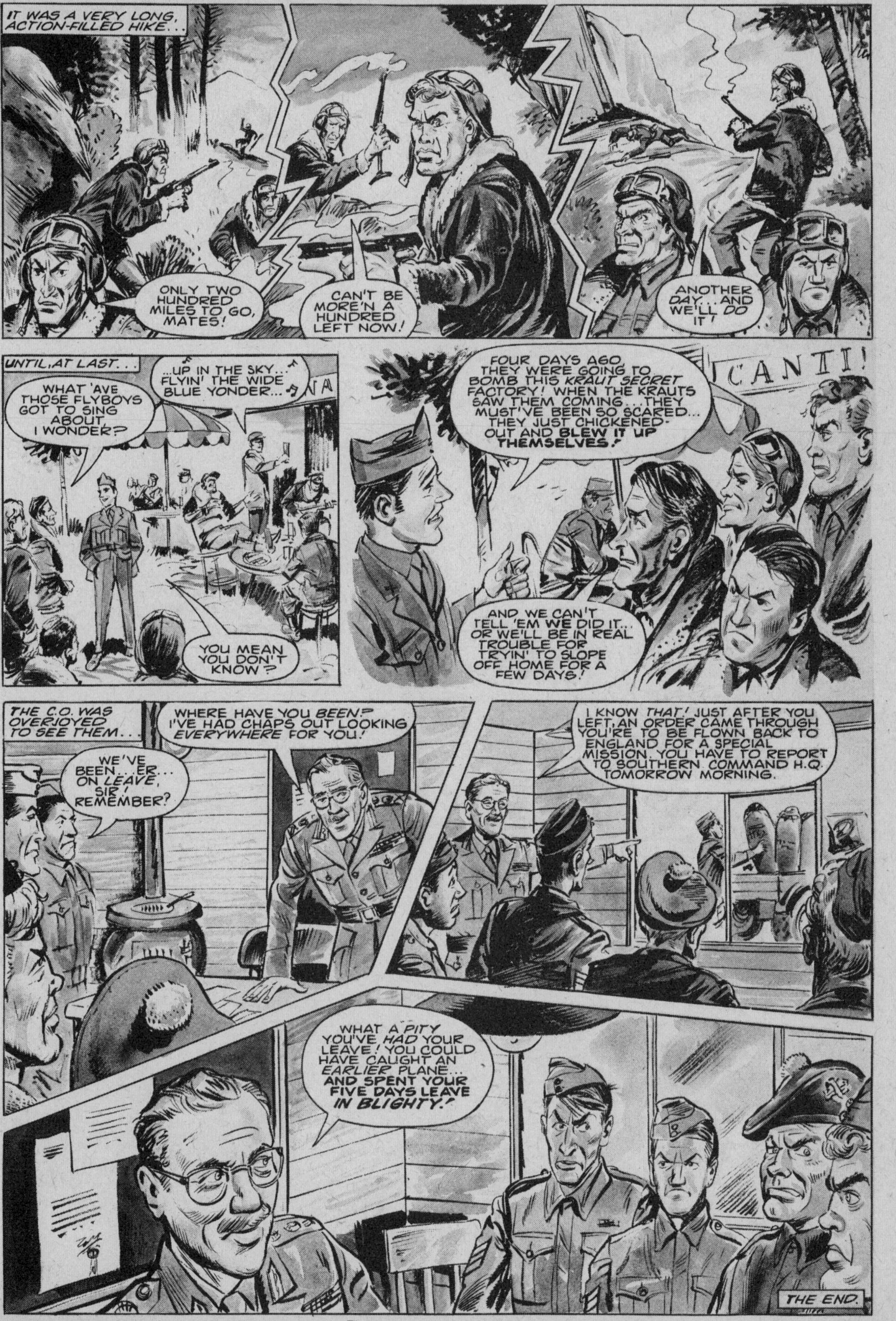

THE C.O. WAS OVERJOYED TO SEE THEM...

WHERE HAVE YOU *BEEN?* I'VE HAD CHAPS OUT LOOKING *EVERYWHERE* FOR YOU!

WE'VE BEEN... ER... ON *LEAVE*, SIR! REMEMBER?

I KNOW *THAT!* JUST AFTER YOU LEFT, AN ORDER CAME THROUGH YOU'RE TO BE FLOWN BACK TO ENGLAND FOR A SPECIAL MISSION. YOU HAVE TO REPORT TO SOUTHERN COMMAND H.Q. TOMORROW MORNING.

WHAT A *PITY* YOU'VE *HAD* YOUR LEAVE! YOU COULD HAVE CAUGHT AN *EARLIER* PLANE... **AND SPENT YOUR FIVE DAYS LEAVE *IN BLIGHTY!***

THE END.

Bertie
Bumpkin

BERTIE WAS HELPING FARMER FURROWFIELD GATHER HAY ON A RIVERSIDE MEADOW...
GOOD WORK, BERTIE! YOU'RE A REAL HELP!
ALWAYS 'APPY TO 'ELP OUT A NEIGHBOUR, SQUOIRE!

GREAT! THE FARMER'S ALONE... 'CEPT FOR ONE DOPEY-LOOKING YOKEL!
THE FARMER SHOULD BE GOOD FOR A FEW QUID!
WELL, MURBLE MY WATTLESNOCKS... WE'VE GOT VISITORS!

HANDS UP! HAND OVER YOUR WALLET... AN' NO ONE GETS HURT!
GOOR! YOU DON'T FROIGHTEN ME WITH THAT POP-GUN! BE OFF WITH YOU..!
I'LL DEAL WITH THIS BLOKE, SIMON!

GET THE POINT? YERK, YERK!
YEEEEEAGH!
PROYING!
WHAMPF!

BUT BERTIE WAS STILL ON THE WARPATH...
OI'M A'GOIN' TO LUMP YER 'EADS, YOU NO-GOOD CROOK-FELLERS!
TWIT! HE'S STILL AT IT... WE'LL HAVE TO GET TOUGH!
I'LL FIX HIM THIS TIME..!

THERE! HE'LL NOT GET DOWN IN A HURRY!
HELP I'VE BEEN ROBBED!
LET'S GET BACK TO THE BOAT, MARTIN!

THE FARMER'S CRIES SOON BROUGHT A COUPLE OF FARM-LADS RUSHING TO THE SCENE...
SOON HAVE YOU UNTIED, SIR!
DOO! OI CAN'T GET DOWN...
GAAAH! WHAT'S THE USE? THOSE ROGUES HAVE GOT AWAY WITH MY WALLET!

WITHOUT A BOAT TO FOLLOW THEM, WE DON'T STAND A CHANCE OF CATCHING THE SCOUNDRELS.!
OH, YUS WE DO, SQUOIRE! OI'VE GOT AN OIDEA! YOU LADS GRAB 'OLD OF ME FEET AND PULL OI BACKWARDS AS FAR AS YOU CAN!

ROIGHT, LADS! LET 'ER GO!
B-E-E-E-ND!

GEER-TWANNNNNNG!
HERE OI COME!
WELL I NEVER...!
A CLEAN GETAWAY, MARTIN! TEE, HEE!

WAAAAHAAAY! BULLSEYE!
GURK!
THUNK!

BRAVE FELLOW! I'LL SEE YOU'RE WELL REWARDED FOR THIS!
GROAN! WHAT HIT ME?
TWO CROOKS- TOGETHER WITH LOOT- COMIN' UP, SQUOIRE!

THE speeding police patrol car screamed round yet another bend in the winding country road. The driver just glimpsed the car he was chasing.

"He's still ahead, Larry," he gasped to his companion, "exceeding the speed limit, and driving like a maniac!"

"We'll throw the book at this one when we catch him, Bert! Stolen car . . . breaking every rule of the road! Look, the nut's still driving on the right hand side!"

Patrolman Bert Adams scowled. "We'll get him! But if we don't, there's another car waiting at the cross-roads before Little Twittering! Every car on the radio net's after that geezer since he stole that Todd Tornado from the town square at Milchester! *Cor, what a nut-case!*"

Both policemen were near the mark in their estimation of the car thief. For crouched at the wheel, swinging it wildly, his foot hard down on the accelerator pedal, was Doktor Von Hoffman, hair flying, wild-eyed, a German scientist who had become crazed with the idea of revenge against Britain after twenty-five years in prison for war crimes.

Inventor of a gas which enlarged all animals and insects and caused them to do his bidding, Von Hoffman had come on a one-man invasion to destroy Britain.

Hooked over his arm was the umbrella which was really a powerful spray container for his deadly gas.

Glittering eyes flickered to the rear-view mirror.

"Ach, the so-stupid Englischer police still think they can catch the great Von Hoffman," he screamed wildly. "I vill from them get avay!"

The tyres of the powerful Todd Tornado saloon screamed as he swung it into yet another side road.

"The so-secret aircraft establishment near Little Twittering iss my objective!" he yelled to himself. "Nothing vill stop me destroying it!"

Flat out, he raced along on the right-hand side of the narrow country road, glimpsing the police car turning after him. Coming towards him was an old truck driven by a sleepy farmer.

The Tornado's horn blared as Von Hoffman's gnarled hand slammed against it.

"These Britischers are so stupid!" he raved. "Vy must dey alvays drive on der wrong side of der road?"

He hurled the car like a bullet at the oncoming vehicle.

White-faced, yelling insults, the farmer saw just in time that the crazy driver coming towards him did not intend to give way. He swung the steering wheel wildly, swerved to the right of the road, shot up a bank and bumped into a field with pieces of hedge scattered over his car.

"See that, Larry?" barked Bert Adams. "Another witness if we want one!"

Von Hoffman had vanished. He swung the car into a narrow track and bumped furiously along it. Then he saw a hollow to his right, braked with skidding wheels, and leapt out with his umbrella to allow the stolen car to dive into the hollow, turn over and over, and crumple with a rending of metal and splintering of glass.

"Hee, hee!" screeched Von Hoffman as he scuttled into a wood at the other side of the road. "By der time der Britischer idiots in blue haf investigated der auto, I shall be far avay!"

Running, the crazy scientist lurched against a

rotting tree, and recoiled. He heard a deep and angry buzz, and striped insects swarmed out towards him. Von Hoffman staggered back as they zoomed at him, but then his umbrella came up, and from its nozzle spurted a cloud of his fantastic gas.

"A nest of hornets I haf disturbed," he crowed. "Wunderbar! Kolossal! With my gas, they vill become Von Hoffman's own Luftwaffe!"

The effect on the swarm of hornets was instantaneous. They swelled to the size of fighter planes, and their angry humming rose to a deafening roar, louder than the engines of a squadron of jets. Exultantly, Von Hoffman waved an arm.

"Attack, my beauties!" he screeched. "Drive those polizei avay. Den another task I shall haf for you!"

Braking to investigate the crashed car in the hollow, Bert Adams and his colleague, white-faced, rolled the car windows shut just in time. They saw the hornets diving on them, darkening the sky, like a swarm of fighter planes.

"For Pete's sake!" yelled Larry. "Put your foot down, Bert. Let's get away! I've never seen anything like it . . . hornets, big as planes. They'd smash our windows if they hit 'em!"

The police car accelerated away, pursued by the giant hornets, until Von Hoffman scuttled from cover, chuckling, and called off his amazing squadron.

"From them dere will no further trouble be," he howled. "Come, my beauties! To Little Twittering! The village I vill take over, and another auto I vill find!"

The hornet swarm circled, and Von Hoffman, following at a tireless run, with his hair flowing wildly, saw them swoop like dive-bombers on the sleepy village. People caught outside ran for their lives, seeking cover in hedges and coppices. Those indoors slammed doors and windows shut, and cowered, hands over ears to shut out the deafening roar.

Windows shattered as the giant hornets smashed against them, but the insects were too big to get into the houses, and the sturdy brick and stone buildings stood up against their onslaught. The occupants, dazed and panicking, retreated to inner rooms. But Von Hoffman, running down the empty main street, cheered as he saw one huge hornet smash into a wooden barn and bring it tumbling down in a shower of splintered wood.

"Von Hoffman strikes!" he crowed. "Little Twittering will never forget the might of Nazi Germany's most noble scientist!"

Those who still ventured to peer out of windows saw the crazily-capering little man run to a sturdy baker's van parked outside the village store. At roof level, the mighty hornets menaced the village in high-speed runs like strafing fighter planes.

But even as Von Hoffman started the van's engine, they saw an amazing sight. The hornets dwindled, shrank to their normal size, formed up into a swarm again, and went buzzing away.

"Ach, so," snarled Von Hoffman. "The effect of ze gas has worn off. Vun day when I time haf, I vill

The swarm of giant hornets circled, then swooped like dive-bombers on the village.

perfect it so that it is everlasting. Den der accursed Britischers vill cause to tremble haf!"

The mad scientist slammed in the clutch and the van roared away. But now angry villagers were running out, leaping into cars and on to scooters and motor-bikes to give chase.

"Fools! Dummkopfs!" screeched Von Hoffman. "You vill not stop me reaching my objective!"

Driving furiously, he kept the van ahead of his pursuers until he lurched on two wheels into a narrow forest track and sped along it, bumping against trees on either side. Then he saw a high wire fence ahead of him, and drove straight at it.

"I haf arrived!" he yelled. "This is der secret establishment. All I need now is to find der animals and other creatures to assist me in its destruction!"

Recklessly, he smashed the van through the wire fence, and drove with wire trailing across a stretch of open grassland. Then his jaw dropped and his eyes rolled angrily.

"Himmel! Dis is not der aircraft establishment. *To der wrong place I haf komm!*"

Safari Park

For one wild moment Von Hoffman thought he had landed suddenly in a foreign country—some far-off tropical place like Africa or India.

As he drove, he saw elephants trundling placidly among the scattered trees, a group of lions padding regally across the grass, a sleepy leopard stretched along a tree trunk, and a tall giraffe turning its head lazily, while cropping leaves, to stare incuriously at the oncoming van.

Two tigers loped ahead of him, and he saw monkeys swinging high in some of the trees.

"Himmel!" he moaned, rubbing his eyes. "Der strain it is too much. I am out of my mind going!"

But then he saw a distant sign, a huge board raised on concrete columns, and read: "COPPERFIELD'S SAFARI PARK". He saw lines of cars driving slowly along a road with windows closed, as the occupants watched the roaming animals.

"Ach, it iss one of der places where the mad Englischers let vild animals roam free," he chuckled. "Himmel, dey have played into my hands. Such friends for Von Hoffman . . . such beautiful vild friends!"

Delightedly, the crazed Nazi leapt out of the van and ran scuttling among the animals, squirting gas from his umbrella. The effect was even better than he had hoped. Elephants grew bigger than houses. Lions, tigers, and other animals enlarged to alarming and menacing size.

At Von Hoffman's order, a giant elephant, far bigger than a prehistoric mammoth, lifted him with its trunk and set him down to squat on its broad head.

"Forward! Forward! Attack, my beauties!" he screeched, and the whole giant herd surged forward. "Now ve vill der aircraft place find, and destroy it!"

Faced by the herd of monstrous animals, car drivers had panicked and were driving off in all directions, scattering across the huge park, passengers screaming in fright.

A warden, white-faced, watched the oncoming herd, and raised his rifle. Then he lowered it, and dived for cover into a handy pit.

"Stone me, bullets would be useless against that mob!" he gasped. "They'd just bounce off those oversize elephants! I'd think I was imagining things, if those car drivers weren't scarpering, too! What the heck's happened to the beasts?"

Only Von Hoffman could have told him that. Perched like a tiny doll high between the elephant's flapping ears, the scientist was chuckling with fiendish glee, unseen by any of the fleeing spectators of the amazing transformation scene.

Bellowing, roaring, the wild animal herd smashed down the gates to the Safari Park, trampling an

Von Hoffman's incredible zoo charged through the electrified fence . . . and guard dogs fled in terror before them. . . .

abandoned car flat, and surged down the main road outside.

Ahead of him, Von Hoffman saw an airfield and scattered buildings beyond a high wire fence, with a sign: "MINISTRY OF DEFENCE. KEEP OUT!"

"Onward, my beauties!" roared Von Hoffman. "Nothing vill keep us out!"

Elephants smashed through the fence, and blue flame flickered like lightning, as, undaunted under Von Hoffman's spell, the whole herd followed. The electrified fence could not stop the giant elephants, and guard dogs that had been prowling inside fled yowling in panic, followed by their white-faced handlers.

Von Hoffman's army of wild beasts raced across the airfield, the ground shaking beneath their pads and hoofs. He saw an aircraft, an advanced strike-fighter, parked on the concrete apron outside some hangars, its jets whistling as the engines were warmed up.

Giant herd

Mechanics halted in their work, stared, then ran as Von Hoffman directed the herd towards it. The pilot, walking towards it, just putting on his domed helmet, stopped, petrified, then turned and ran for the shelter of the hangars.

All around the airfield and from the research buildings, alarm klaxons shrilled. But Von Hoffman's elephant thundered towards the jet plane.

Its trunk curled down, and Von Hoffman's weird laughter rang above the shriek of the jets as the elephant picked up the plane and hurled it like a toy hundreds of feet through the air. It landed with a crumpling crash, like a smashed matchbox, burst into flame and exploded, a ball of smoke and flame roaring up towards the sky.

"Wunderbar!" shrieked Von Hoffman. "I haf der secret plane destroyed! Now . . . now . . . my so lovely friends, ve vill wreck the buildings and destroy der man whose brains haf built it!"

Appalled by the instant destruction of the plane which had taken years of planning and months of construction to bring to its flight tests, scientists and other workers gaped at the herd as it turned towards the buildings.

Security guards opened fire with machine-guns and rifles, but the bullets hummed with little effect among the monster animals. Some fell, howling, but the majority stormed onwards, as Von Hoffman pointed to a long, low, concrete building with large windows.

"Dat is der secret laboratory!" he howled. "Ve vill go through it like a typhoon. Nothing but rubble and shreds of glass vill remain!"

Seeing their danger, the occupants were crowding to the entrance of the vast underground radar and control rooms which had been built to withstand a nuclear blast. Nothing, it seemed, could stop the onrush of the animals—the vicious, menacing attack of Von Hoffman's fantastic army.

A few men were still standing their ground, shooting, in a futile attempt to halt the giants.

Then, suddenly, they saw an amazing sight, even as they prepared to retreat, every man for himself. . . .

The animals dwindled. Men rubbed their eyes as they saw the monsters shrink to normal size. More, the animals panicked as they heard gunfire crackling. Accustomed to the peaceful lives they had led in the safari park, they now faced man and all his dangers again.

Trumpeting in fear, Von Hoffman's shrunken elephant veered away, and the crazed scientist, yelling in frustrated fury, was hurled from his perch to land with a bone-shaking thud inside a concrete engine-testing bay.

"Donner und Blitzen!" he screamed. "I haf been foiled! Again the effect of my beautiful gas has worn off."

Screaming to the sky, he saw the animal herd

racing back across the airfield as wardens in trucks, with nets and rifles, sped to head them off.

Von Hoffman's mightiest blow against the hated British had failed with only seconds to go before complete destruction of the secret base.

Gnashing his teeth, his hands twitching, he prepared to climb out, to escape if he could. Men with rifles were running, looking for him, for some had seen the tiny figure fall off the elephant.

Then he heard a whimper beside him. He looked down and his eyes glittered as he saw a frightened mongrel dog cowering in a corner of the bay, where it had taken refuge from the mammoth herd.

Instantly, Von Hoffman's umbrella squirted gas.

"You vill your day haf, my beauty," the scientist crowed. "You vill the honour haf of saving the great Von Hoffman so that he can continue his fight against the evil Britischers who defeated der Fatherland!"

He jumped up as the dog swelled to enormous size. Obeying his order, it leapt out of the bay and bounded away across the airfield.

Running men halted, rifles held in paralysed hands, as they saw the giant dog racing away with enormous strides, Von Hoffman, tiny on its neck, clutching its ruff of hair.

"For Pete's sake," cried one of the men. "D'you see what I see? It's a dog . . . a perishing dog as big as a flamin' house. It came from that engine-bay! But it couldn't have . . . it's not possible! It'd never have fitted into it!"

Cackling, Von Hoffman sped on his giant steed across fields and over hills. He exulted in the destruction he had left behind him. The aircraft research men, glad that the second prototype of the experimental plane was secure in a hangar; the villagers of Little Twittering, still wondering what had hit them; and the baffled policemen, still searching for the strange car thief.

But he felt a premonition when the huge hound came to a wide, swift-flowing river. To the dog it looked like a brook and it raced across, splashing through the water . . . until, in midstream—it happened!

"Der Teufel!" howled Von Hoffman as the dog suddenly shrank to normal size, and he was hurled into the water!

Yelping, the dog swam to the far bank, but Von Hoffman, clutching his umbrella, was swept away. He had gone half a mile downstream, and was half-drowned, when he crawled, dripping, on to a spit of land.

With water pouring from his wild hair and his wrinkled clothes, the crazed scientist danced squelchingly on the river bank, his hands shaking above his head.

"Donner und Blitzen, that this should happen to me, the great Von Hoffman!" he howled. "Ach, the infernal Englanders shall pay for this! I shall my vengeance wreak! The pigdogs have yet to feel der full weight of Von Hoffman's war to the death!"

The mighty tusker picked up the jet-plane and hurled it far away. It exploded in a ball of fire and smoke.

? DO YOU KNOW ?

1. Can you tell from this picture which way the tide is flowing ?

2. There's something important missing from this map of Australasia. What is it ?

3. Is the baseball player indicated by the arrow called a wicket-keeper, catcher or a stopper ?

4. Does a Bombay Duck nest in " A " or " B " ?

5. Can you identify the two aircraft shown below ?

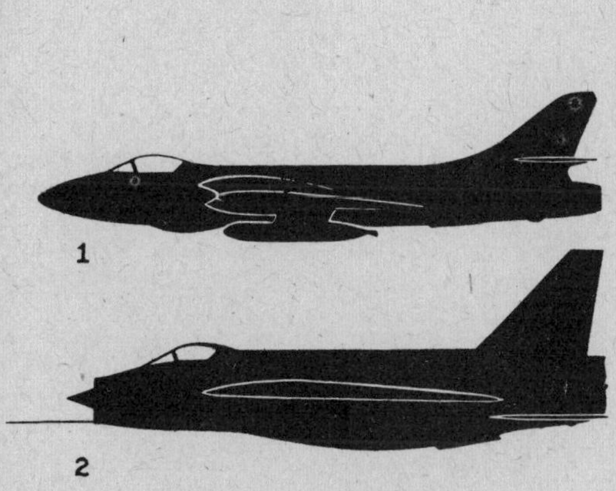

6. Are unicorns ever seen doing this ?

7. Is this a viaduct or an aqueduct ?

8. Is he in the North West Mounted Police, the Royal North West Mounted Police, or the Royal Canadian Mounted Police ?

ANSWERS TO THE QUIZ

(Turn the page upside-down to read them.)

1. From right to left of the picture ; See the water round the pier post, and the direction of the ship's anchor chain.
2. The island of Tasmania, off Australia's south coast.
3. Catcher. 4. Neither. The Bombay Duck is a fish ;
5. Upper (1) Hawker Hunter F.MK.6 ; lower (2) English Electric Lightning F.MK.3.
6. No, because there is no such animal as a unicorn, except in legends.
7. A viaduct. 8. The Royal Canadian Mounted Police.

PADDY
McGINTY'S GOAT

YOUNG PADDY McGINTY HAD FOUND A FRIENDLY CREATURE FROM OUTER SPACE WHO COULD TAKE ON THE APPEARANCE OF ANY OTHER ANIMAL. AT PADDY'S SUGGESTION, THE CREATURE CHANGED HIMSELF INTO A GOAT. JUST BEFORE CHRISTMAS PADDY AND HIS WONDERFUL GOAT TOOK A TRIP TO THE LAKE DISTRICT...
WELL, WE'VE SEEN LAKE NOSS, GOAT. BUT NO MONSTER! I TOLD YOU IT WAS JUST A FAIRY TALE!
PITY THAT, PADDY! I'D LIKE TO SEE WHAT A REAL EARTHLING MONSTER IS LIKE!

ANYWAY YOU CAN SEE REAL ANIMALS WHEN WE GET TO THE ZOO.
ZOO
YOU MEAN LIONS AND TIGERS AND SUCH. THAT'LL BE INTERESTING. I'VE ONLY SEEN SOME OF THEM IN YOUR ANIMAL BOOK!

BUT WHEN THEY GOT THERE...
THERE... THERE'S NOTHING THERE!
THAT'S RIGHT, MATE! THE ZOO CLOSED UP! TEEE HEEEE... IT GIVES ME A REAL GIGGLE IT DOES... WATCHIN' PEOPLE'S FACES WHEN THEY FIND OUT!

YOU SHOULD SEE THE DISAPPOINTMENT ON THEIR FACES! TEEEE-HEEE! A PROPER LAUGH, IT IS!
PADDY, I THOUGHT YOU SAID CHRISTMAS WAS A TIME OF GOODWILL!.. WHEN YOU TRIED TO BE ESPECIALLY NICE TO OTHER PEOPLE..!
IT'S ROTTEN BLOKES LIKE HIM THAT SPOIL CHRISTMAS, GOAT.
NEVER MIND, PADDY! WE'LL TRY AND HAND OUT AN EXTRA BIT OF GOODWILL TO MAKE UP FOR HIM!

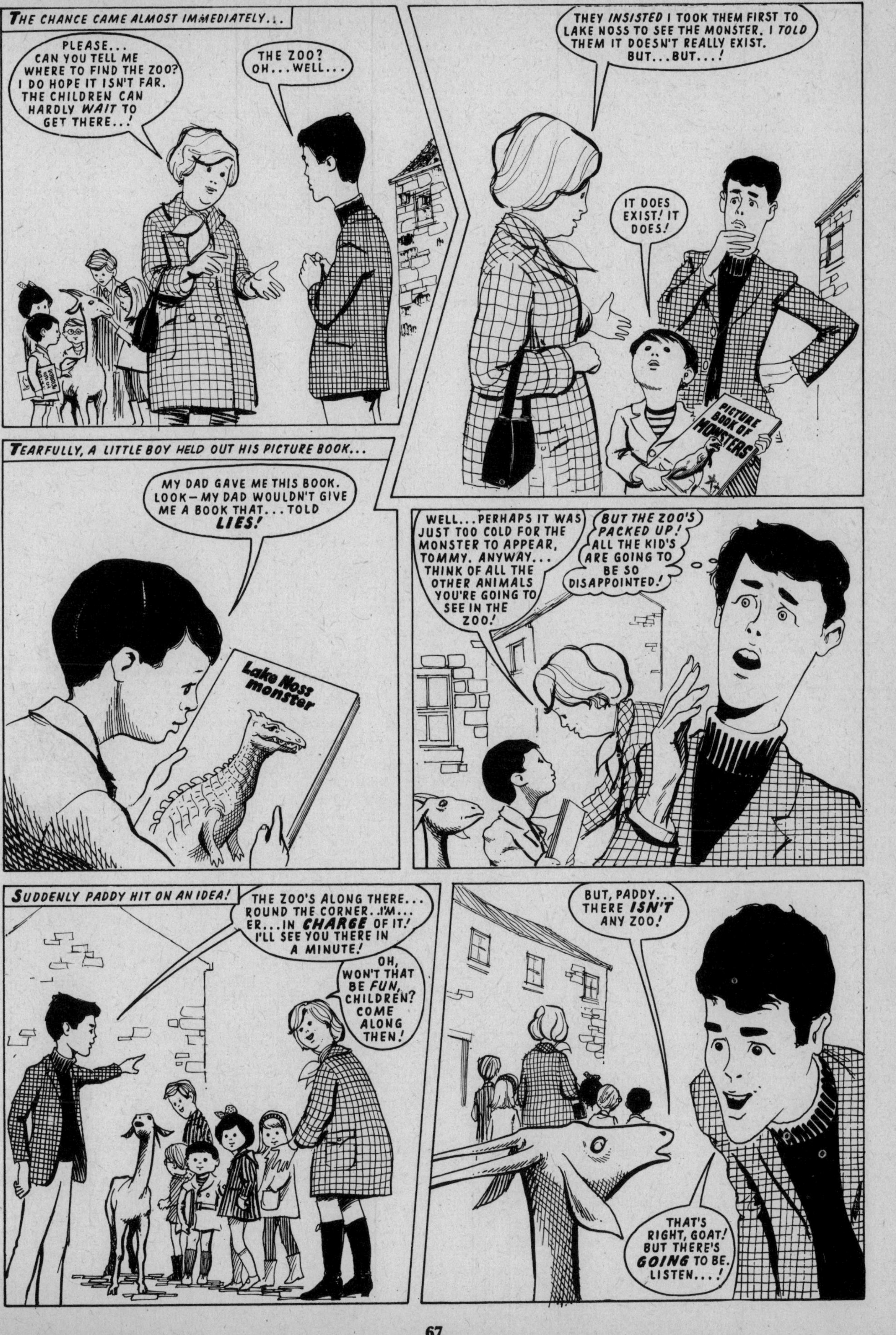

THE CHANCE CAME ALMOST IMMEDIATELY...

PLEASE... CAN YOU TELL ME WHERE TO FIND THE ZOO? I DO HOPE IT ISN'T FAR. THE CHILDREN CAN HARDLY *WAIT* TO GET THERE...!

THE ZOO? OH... WELL...

THEY *INSISTED* I TOOK THEM FIRST TO LAKE NOSS TO SEE THE MONSTER. I *TOLD* THEM IT DOESN'T REALLY EXIST. BUT... BUT...!

IT DOES EXIST! IT DOES!

PICTURE BOOK OF MONSTERS

TEARFULLY, A LITTLE BOY HELD OUT HIS PICTURE BOOK...

MY DAD GAVE ME THIS BOOK. LOOK—MY DAD WOULDN'T GIVE ME A BOOK THAT... TOLD **LIES!**

Lake Noss monster

WELL... PERHAPS IT WAS JUST TOO COLD FOR THE MONSTER TO APPEAR, TOMMY. ANYWAY... THINK OF ALL THE OTHER ANIMALS YOU'RE GOING TO SEE IN THE ZOO!

BUT THE ZOO'S PACKED UP! ALL THE KID'S ARE GOING TO BE SO DISAPPOINTED!

SECONDS LATER...
BAAAAAA! THAT'S A GREAT IDEA, PADDY! I'LL GO THIS WAY, AND GET TO THE ZOO FIRST... WITHOUT THEM SEEING ME!
GOOD! THEN THEY WON'T SUSPECT A THING!
PADDY CAUGHT UP WITH THE PARTY JUST BEFORE THEY ENTERED THE GATES...
THIS WAY! I'M SORRY I'M NOT WEARING MY KEEPER'S UNIFORM. BUT THAT WON'T STOP YOU ENJOYING THE ANIMALS, WILL IT?
COR STREWTH... YOU'RE A COOL ONE, MATE!
TEEEE HEEEE! YOU'RE A REAL CARD, YOU ARE! REALLY HAVIN' 'EM ON, AIN'T YOU? CAN'T WAIT TO SEE THEIR POOR LITTLE FACES WHEN THEY COME OUT! TEEE-HEEEE! I WISH I'D THOUGHT OF THAT ONE!
IT... IT ISN'T VERY CROWDED, IS IT?
ALL THE BETTER TO SEE THE ANIMALS PROPERLY.
LION
GOT TO HURRY UP AND CHANGE INTO A LION BEFORE THEY GET HERE!
FOR A SPLIT SECOND THE GOAT BECAME THE CREATURE FROM OUTER SPACE THAT PADDY HAD FIRST ENCOUNTERED MANY MONTHS BEFORE...
MUST SWITCH TO MY REAL SHAPE FIRST...!
THEN...
THERE! THAT DOES IT!
EEK! THE LION'S CAGE DOOR IS OPEN!
OF COURSE IT IS, MADAM! WE DON'T KEEP OUR ANIMALS LOCKED UP IN THIS ZOO! THEY'RE MUCH TOO FRIENDLY FOR THAT!
AND SO IT SEEMED...
HOW WONDERFUL FOR THEM!
LOOK! HE'S LICKING ME!
OH, HE'S SUPER!
THIS WAY NOW... COME ON!

QUICKLY THE CREATURE-FROM-SPACE CHANGED AGAIN...
NOW WE'RE GOING TO SEE THE GORILLA! AND HE'S JUST AS FRIENDLY AS THAT LION!
PHEW! THIS IS HARD WORK. BUT WORTH IT!
LION
WHEEEEEEEE! ISN'T HE NICE! NOT FIERCE AT ALL!
HOW AM I DOING, PADDY?
GREAT! KEEP IT UP!
AND PADDY'S WONDERFUL GOAT DID...
PHEW! PADDY, I'VE NEVER DONE SO MUCH CHANGING IN ONE DAY!
BUT AS YOU SAID... IT'S WORTH IT, GOAT! LOOK AT THE HAPPINESS YOU'RE GIVING THEM!
AT LAST...
OH, THAT WAS SUPER! HEY...WHERE'S YOUR GOAT?
OH HE'S AROUND!
HUH? THEY...THEY'RE LOOKING HAPPY! I...I DON'T GET IT!
HERE'S YOUR GOAT! I WONDER WHERE HE'S BEEN?
PLEASE... COULDN'T YOU HELP US SEE THE LAKE NOSS MONSTER?
TEEEEE-HEEEEE! NOW WATCH THEIR FACES DROP!

OH YES, PLEASE!
WHAT DO YOU SAY, GOAT! CAN YOU DO IT?
'COURSE I CAN! I SAW THE PICTURE IN TOMMY'S BOOK... SO I KNOW WHAT IT'S SUPPOSED TO LOOK LIKE. JUST GIVE ME TIME TO GET TO THE LAKE FIRST!
WHEN PADDY'S GOAT HAD DISAPPEARED...
SURE I'LL SHOW YOU THE MONSTER. WE'LL GO TO THE LAKE RIGHT NOW!
TEEEEE-HEEEEE! I DUNNO WHAT HAPPENED BEFORE... BUT HE'S LEADIN' THEM RIGHT UP THE OLD GARDEN PATH NOW! LUVLY!

I...I KNOW YOU MEAN WELL. BUT I WON'T COME WITH YOU. I...I COULDN'T BEAR TO SEE THEIR DISAPPOINTED FACES AGAIN..!
ALL RIGHT, MADAM! PERHAPS IT'S JUST AS WELL!
AS THE PARTY WALKED TOWARDS LAKE NOSS...
BRRRR! IT LOOKS COLD! BUT I MUST GO ON WITH IT... SPECIALLY AS IT'S CHRISTMAS. NOW WHAT DID THAT PICTURE IN TOMMY'S BOOK LOOK LIKE?... AH YES, I REMEMBER!

GOT TO CHANGE TO MY REAL SELF FIRST. THAT'S IT! AND NOW..!

...HEY PRESTO! INSTANT MONSTER!

FIVE MINUTES LATER...
WHERE IS IT?
I CAN'T SEE IT!
YOU WEREN'T FIBBING WERE YOU? THE MONSTER REALLY IS HERE... ISN'T HE?
HE IS, PROVIDED GOAT DIDN'T FIND THIS CHANGE TOO MUCH FOR HIM!

THEN SUDDENLY...
PHEW! GOOD OLD GOAT!
THERE HE IS!
I TOLD YOU! I TOLD YOU!

THERE FOLLOWED AN EXHIBITION THE CHILDREN WERE NEVER TO FORGET...
LOOK! HE...HE'S PUTTING ON A SHOW FOR US!
ISN'T HE A SUPER MONSTER?
UNTIL AT LAST...
HE'S DIVING UNDER!
GOODBYE, MONSTER!
ENOUGH'S ENOUGH! EVEN MONSTER'S GET TIRED EVENTUALLY!

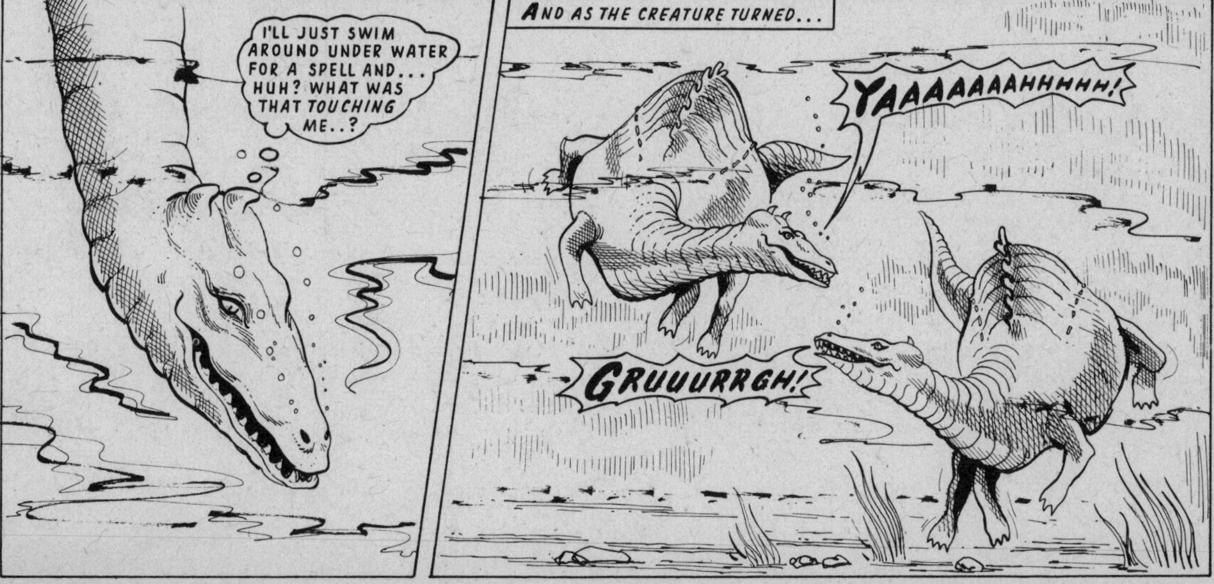
I'LL JUST SWIM AROUND UNDER WATER FOR A SPELL AND... HUH? WHAT WAS THAT TOUCHING ME..?
AND AS THE CREATURE TURNED...
YAAAAAAAHHHHH!
GRUUURRGH!

ONE QUICK LOOK WAS ENOUGH FOR THE CREATURE-FROM-SPACE...

THERE HE IS AGAIN.

HE'S MAKING FOR THAT BAY OVER THERE!

COME ON! WE MAY BE ABLE TO SEE HIM CLOSER!

BUT ALL THEY FOUND WAS PADDY McGINTY'S GOAT...

YOUR GOAT'S ALL WET, MISTER! HE MUST HAVE BEEN IN THE LAKE! HE LOOKS SCARED!

GOAT! WHAT IS IT?

PADDY... YOU DON'T HAVE TO WORRY ABOUT TELLING ANY *UNTRUTHS* ABOUT THERE REALLY BEING A LAKE NOSS MONSTER..!

YOU MEAN...YOU MEAN..? **GGGGGGOSH!**

AND SO...

THE ZOO,...AND THEN THE MONSTER! IT'S BEEN THE BEST CHRISTMAS OUTING WE EVER HAD!

OH IT WAS WONDERFUL. WE SAW IT... WE SAW IT!

I...I DON'T KNOW HOW TO THANK YOU. I DON'T KNOW HOW YOU *DID* IT... BUT IF ANYONE EVER EARNED A MERRY CHRISTMAS FOR THEMSELVES IT'S ***YOU!***

AND GOAT! *HE* DID ALL THE WORK!

YOU KNOW I *LIKE* CHRISTMAS, PADDY. ESPECIALLY WHEN YOU CAN GIVE LOTS OF GOOD WILL!

I...I DON'T GET IT! I...JUST...DON'T... *GET* IT!

THE END

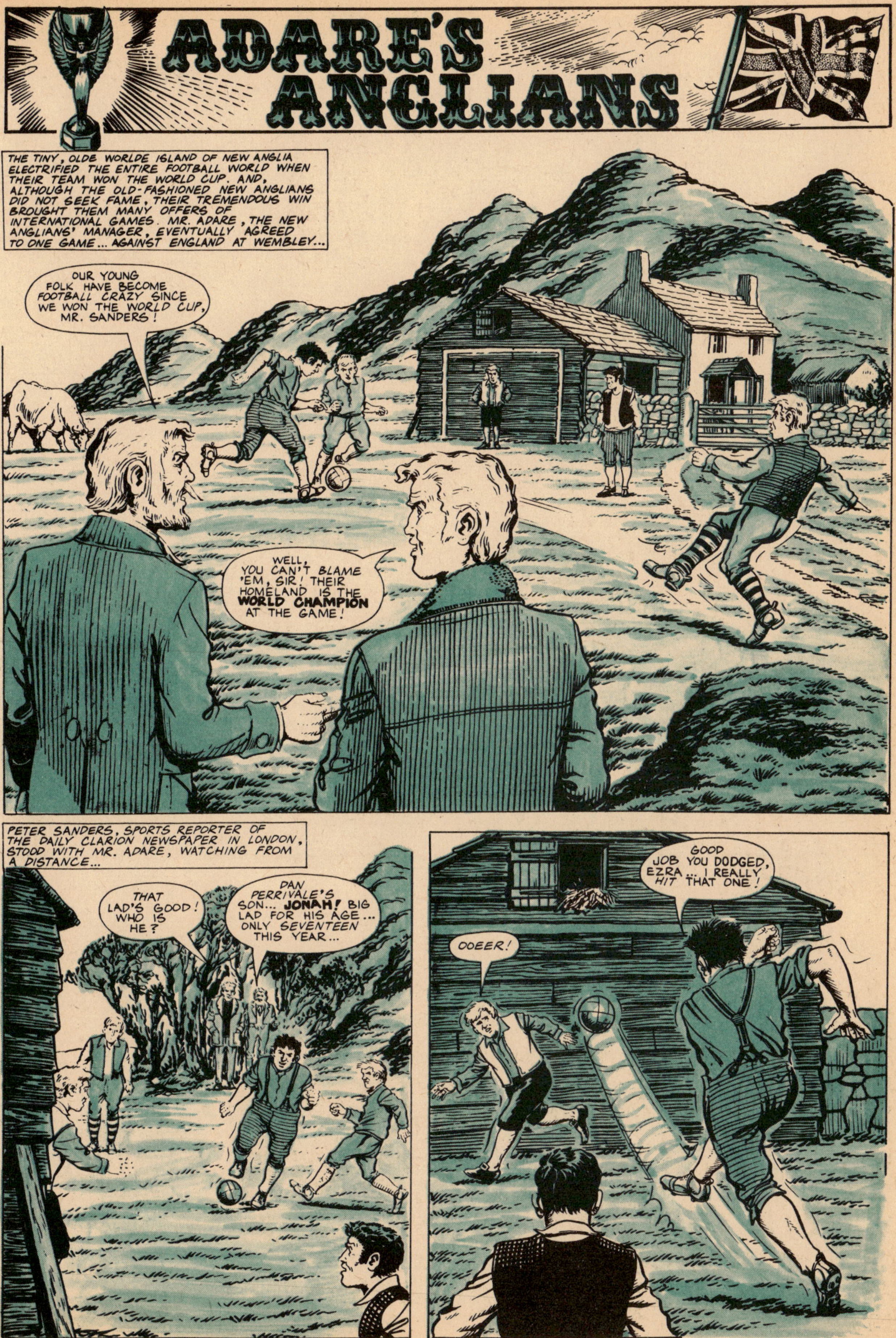

ADARE'S ANGLIANS

THE TINY, OLDE WORLDE ISLAND OF NEW ANGLIA ELECTRIFIED THE ENTIRE FOOTBALL WORLD WHEN THEIR TEAM WON THE WORLD CUP. AND, ALTHOUGH THE OLD-FASHIONED NEW ANGLIANS DID NOT SEEK FAME, THEIR TREMENDOUS WIN BROUGHT THEM MANY OFFERS OF INTERNATIONAL GAMES. MR. ADARE, THE NEW ANGLIANS' MANAGER, EVENTUALLY AGREED TO ONE GAME... AGAINST ENGLAND AT WEMBLEY...

OUR YOUNG FOLK HAVE BECOME FOOTBALL CRAZY SINCE WE WON THE WORLD CUP, MR. SANDERS!

WELL, YOU CAN'T BLAME 'EM, SIR! THEIR HOMELAND IS THE **WORLD CHAMPION** AT THE GAME!

PETER SANDERS, SPORTS REPORTER OF THE DAILY CLARION NEWSPAPER IN LONDON, STOOD WITH MR. ADARE, WATCHING FROM A DISTANCE...

NEWS OF THE DISASTER REACHED LONDON, AND THE FOOTBALL ASSOCIATION CALLED A HURRIED MEETING...

FORTUNATELY, NO ONE WAS KILLED... BUT FOUR OF THE SHIP'S CREW WERE INJURED AND ALL OF THEM WERE MEMBERS OF NEW ANGLIA'S **WORLD CUP TEAM!**

WE'LL OFFER TO CANCEL THE GAME AGAINST ENGLAND!

YES, I QUITE AGREE!

THE ISLANDERS' REPLY APPEARED ON THE FRONT PAGES OF THE NEWSPAPERS...

clarion
N. ANGLIA HONOURS PROMISE TO PLAY

THE CHRONICLE
WORLD-CUP HOLDERS TO

Daily Ne
WE PLAY

STAR
GAME NOT CANC
SAYS NEW AN

IN NEW ANGLIA, PETE SANDERS QUESTIONED MR. ADARE...
YOU'VE GOT TWO FIRST CLASS RESERVES ... BUT THAT STILL LEAVES TWO MORE PLAYERS! BOTH STRIKERS, TOO ...
I WILL RE-SHUFFLE THE FIRST TEAM MEN! PUT THE NEWCOMERS WHERE THEY CAN BE COVERED...

HEY! HOW ABOUT DAN PERRIVALE'S BOY? WHAT WAS HIS NAME... JONAH? THAT KID HAD A SHOT LIKE A CANNON-BALL!
BY JUPITER... YOU MIGHT BE RIGHT, MR SANDERS!

THEY WENT TO SEE DAN PERRIVALE THAT EVENING. BUT...
MY BOY BELONGS HERE ON THE FARM... NOT KICKING A USELESS LUMP OF LEATHER AROUND! ONE DAY THIS FARM WILL BE HIS... AND HE'LL BE PROUD OF IT... AS I AM! I'M SORRY, MR. ADARE!
I UNDERSTAND YOUR FEELINGS, MR. PERRIVALE!

CAN'T BLAME HIM! THAT FARM MEANS A GREAT DEAL TO HIM!
WE WILL JUST HAVE TO RE-SHUFFLE THE MEN WE HAVE AS BEST WE CAN. WE WILL GIVE ENGLAND A GOOD GAME... WE'RE NOT BEATEN YET!

THREE DAYS LATER, THE NEW ANGLIAN TEAM WERE ABOARD SHIP ON THEIR WAY TO ENGLAND...
WHY YOUR TEAM DON'T FLY TO LONDON, I'LL NEVER KNOW, MR. ADARE! YOU'D GET THERE MUCH QUICKER AND... GROOH! I FEEL ILL!
MOST OF OUR PLAYERS ARE SEAMEN, MR. SANDERS! AND THERE'S NO HURRY! WE'LL BE IN ENGLAND BY DAWN!
ISLAND QUEEN

OHH-OHHHHHH!
WHAT'S THAT?
THERE'S SOMEONE HIDING INSIDE THE LIFEBOAT!

daily clarion

ANGLIANS FIELD NEW WONDER BOY! FIRST GAME IN BIG-TIME FOOTBALL!

IN SPITE OF THE TROUBLES AND NEAR TRAGEDY THAT HAVE BESET THE NEW ANGLIAN TEAM... ENGLAND'S MANAGER SAYS THAT NO QUARTER WILL BE GIVEN AND THE ENGLAND TEAM ARE GOING ALL OUT FOR A BIG WIN OVER THE WORLD CUP-HOLDERS.

THE ENGLISH ARE PLAYING HARD! I WILL SHOW THEM THAT I, TOO... CAN PLAY THAT WAY!
WHEN JONAH RECEIVED HIS NEXT PASS...
HE SAW THAT TACKLE COMING!
SMITHY CAN DISH OUT THE ROUGH STUFF! BUT IT LOOKS AS THOUGH HE'LL BE TAKING SOME BACK!
YEAH! HE GOT THE WORST OF THAT ONE!

JONAH BEAT ANOTHER FIERCE TACKLE...
HE'S THROUGH!
THEY CAN'T STOP HIM, NOW!

GOALLL!
LOVELY SHOT!
WHAT A GOAL! ALL HIS OWN WORK!

BACK IN NEW ANGLIA, DAN WAS TOLD OF HIS SON'S GOAL!
HEY, DAN... YOUR BOY'S JUST SCORED AGAINST ENGLAND! STUPENDOUS SHOT THEY SAID ON THE RADIO...
HUH! YOU SHOULD NOT HAVE BOTHERED TO RIDE OUT TO TELL ME, MASTER HAWKES... I AM NOT INTERESTED IN FOOTBALL!

THE GOAL SCORED AGAINST THEM ROUSED THE ENGLAND SIDE TO THEIR BEST FORM...
OHHHH!
A GOAL'S GOT TO COME... ENGLAND ARE ALL OVER 'EM NOW!

GOALS DID COME... IN THE SECOND HALF!
GOOOALL!
ALL SQUARE — ONE-ALL!

THE CROWD HOWLED FOR THE HOME TEAM...
ENGLAND... ENGLAND... ENGLAND!
LAND

AS THE TEAM RESPONDED MAGNIFICENTLY...
IT'S THERE!
THAT'S IT... ENGLAND'S IN FRONT!
THEY'RE GOING TO BEAT THE CUP-HOLDERS!

I FEEL THAT ENGLAND WILL BEAT US! TIME IS RUNNING SHORT!
EVERY TEAM PLAYS THEIR BEST WHEN MATCHED AGAINST WORLD CUP-HOLDERS... EVERY-ONE WANTS TO BEAT 'EM!
ENGLAND

TWO MINUTES WERE LEFT ON THE CLOCK WHEN JONAH STORMED THROUGH THE ENGLISH DEFENCE!
THERE'S NO OTHER FORWARD UP WITH ME... IF WE'RE GOING TO SCORE... I'VE GOT TO DO IT ALONE!

EVADING TACKLE AFTER TACKLE...
NOW FOR THE SHOT!

THE ENGLISH GOALIE DIDN'T STAND A CHANCE...
GOOALLL!
FANTASTIC!
IT'S A DRAW... THERE'S NO MORE TIME LEFT! HE'S SAVED THE GAME FOR 'EM!

THE FINAL WHISTLE WENT ALMOST IMMEDIATELY...
GREAT GAME, JONAH!
THAT LAST SHOT HAD ME WELL AND TRULY BEAT!
A DRAW WAS A GOOD RESULT... GREAT GAME!

ON THE BOAT BACK TO NEW ANGLIA...
YOU LOOK WORRIED, JONAH ... WHAT'S WRONG?
I'M THINKING OF MY *FATHER*, MR. SANDERS. HE... HE MAY NOT ALLOW ME *BACK HOME*. HE HAS EVERY RIGHT TO REFUSE ME... AFTER *RUNNING* AWAY AS I DID...

WHEN THEY ARRIVED...
LOOK, JONAH ... I'LL GO AHEAD AND *TELL* YOUR DAD *YOU'RE* ON YOUR *WAY*! SMOOTH THINGS OVER A BIT!
NO THANK YOU, SIR... I CAN FACE MY OWN FATHER!

WELL, DO *YOU* THINK HE'LL THROW HIM OUT?
I DON'T *KNOW*, MR. SANDERS! DAN PERRIVALE'S A *HARD MAN*! JUST AND HONEST... BUT A *TOUGH FARMER*!

I'M TOLD YOU'VE BECOME A *NATIONAL HERO*, BOY! PLAYED *WELL* FOR YOUR *COUNTRY*. I EXPECT FARMING'S NOT **GOOD** ENOUGH FOR YOU NOW...
NO, DAD... FARMING'S ALL I WANT TO DO. FOOTBALL IS ONLY A GAME! I WANT TO *WORK* WITH *YOU* AGAIN... IF YOU'LL LET ME!

AYE ... YOU'RE RIGHT, FOOTBALL'S ONLY A GAME! AS LONG AS YOU'VE SENSE TO REALISE THAT... YOU'RE *WELCOME HERE*! **WELCOME HOME, SON!**

A HAPPY ENDING, MR. ADARE!
DAN HAS HIS BOY AGAIN... AND ALTHOUGH NEW ANGLIA'S *LOST* A GOOD **CENTRE-FORWARD**, I'M GLAD IT HAS *ENDED* THIS WAY!
THE END

FACEACHE
SCRUNCH
THE BOY WITH A THOUSAND FACES

NOW DON'T BE SCARED AT WHAT YOU'RE GONNA SEE!

MY IMPERSON-ATION O' THE "PHANTOM O' THE OPERA"!
SCRUNCH

HEH-HEH! NOW TO SWING ABOUT IN THE OLD DISUSED OPERA HOUSE DUE FOR DEMOLITION, AN' SCARE SOMEBODY STIFF!

SO LATER, AT THE DERELICT THEATRE...
HERE WE GO-FROM CIRCLE TO STAGE!

SNAP
YIKES!

STAGE TRAP-DOOR, THROUGH WHICH "DEMON KING" POPS UP.
WHEE-E-E-E!
CRASH

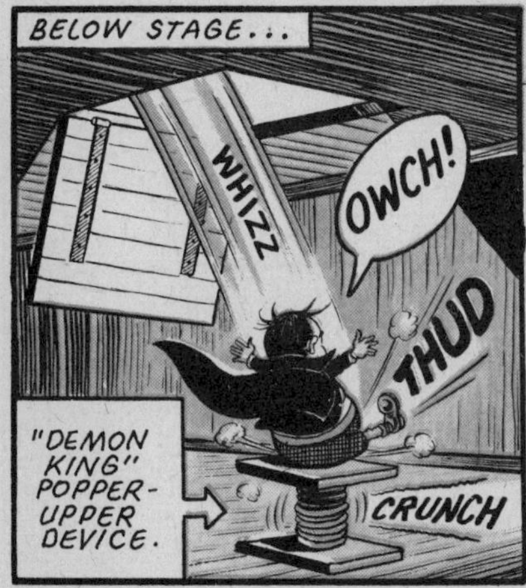
BELOW STAGE...
WHIZZ
OWCH!
THUD
"DEMON KING" POPPER-UPPER DEVICE.
CRUNCH

ZIP
BOYNG

AWLK!
I'VE CHANGED ME MIND ABOUT BEIN' THE "PHANTOM O' THE OPERA"!
SHATTER
OPERA HOU

IT'S TOO DANGEROUS!
FIZZ-Z
AGH!
CRACKLE
FLASH
DANGER
HIGH VOLTAGE

GIBBER-GIBBER-GIBBER-
BANG
LIT UP
FACEACHE'S SUDDEN RISE TO "STARDOM" WAS SHORT-LIVED—

FIZZING FURIOUSLY, HE PLUNGED BACK TO THE OLD OPERA HOUSE —

EEK!
WHOOSH
CRASH
OPERA HOUSE

— VIA THE ROOF...
CLATTER
ZIP
THUD

WHEW! WELL, AT LEAST I LANDED ON A SOFT SEAT! NUTHIN' WORSE CAN HAPPEN TO ME NOW!

BUT THE POOR FRIZZLED LITTLE TWIT DIDN'T KNOW WHAT WAS GOING ON OUTSIDE...
RIGHT, WILF! START DEMOLITION!
OPERA HOUSE
YES, BOSS!
FOR DEMO-LITION

BOOM

WELL DONE, LAD! NOW NIP INSIDE AN' CHECK THAT IT'S SAFE FOR ME TO INSPECT IT!

WILFRED ENTERED THE RUINS...
GIBBER ~ BURBLE ~ BLAH ~ H ~
AWLK!
GROPE

RUN FOR IT! THERE'S SUMMAT IN THERE WOT MAKES THE "PHANTOM O' THE OPERA" LOOK LIKE A ROSE PETAL QUEEN!
!
?

PHANTASHTIC, AIN'T IT! ASH THE "PHANTOM O' THE OPERA" I PHRIGHTENED NOBODY! AN' WHEN I APPEAR ASH ME NORMAL SHELF PEOPLE ARE SHCARED SHTIPH!
SHRIEK!
SCREAM!
I WUNNER WHY?

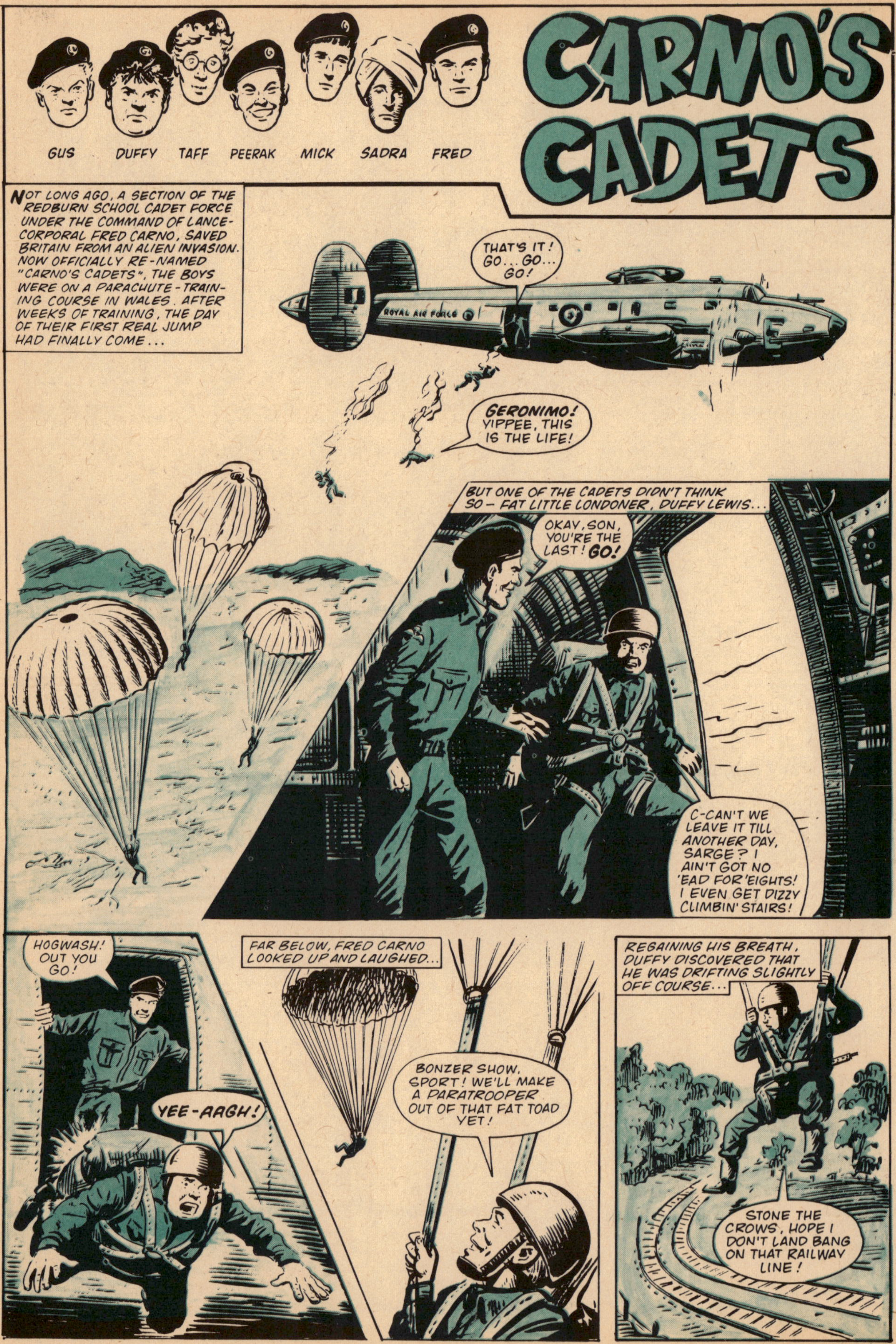

CARNO'S CADETS

NOT LONG AGO, A SECTION OF THE REDBURN SCHOOL CADET FORCE UNDER THE COMMAND OF LANCE-CORPORAL FRED CARNO, SAVED BRITAIN FROM AN ALIEN INVASION. NOW OFFICIALLY RE-NAMED "CARNO'S CADETS", THE BOYS WERE ON A PARACHUTE-TRAINING COURSE IN WALES. AFTER WEEKS OF TRAINING, THE DAY OF THEIR FIRST REAL JUMP HAD FINALLY COME...

THAT'S IT! GO... GO... GO!
ROYAL AIR FORCE
GERONIMO! YIPPEE, THIS IS THE LIFE!

BUT ONE OF THE CADETS DIDN'T THINK SO – FAT LITTLE LONDONER, DUFFY LEWIS...
OKAY, SON, YOU'RE THE LAST! GO!
C-CAN'T WE LEAVE IT TILL ANOTHER DAY, SARGE? I AIN'T GOT NO 'EAD FOR 'EIGHTS! I EVEN GET DIZZY CLIMBIN' STAIRS!

DUFFY LANDED CLOSE TO THE LINE, AND –
FAN ME! THERE'S A LENGTH OF RAIL DETACHED ON THE DOWN-LINE. IT MUST 'AVE WORKED LOOSE SOMEHOW. IF A TRAIN COMES ALONG, IT'LL BE CURTAINS!

QUICKLY, HE TOLD THE OTHER BOYS WHAT HE'D SEEN...
WORKED LOOSE? GAH, YOU'RE SOFT IN THE HEID, LEWIS! RAILS DINNA WORK LOOSE BY THEMSELVES!
I TELL YOU IT'S TRUE, AND IT COULD BE BLOOMIN' DANGEROUS! COME AND SEE FOR YOURSELVES!

SO, MOMENTS LATER...
SINK ME IN A BILABONG, DUFFY, YOU'RE RIGHT! SADRA–YOU AND MICK O'MALLEY RUN UP THE LINE TO THE NEAREST SIGNAL BOX. WARN THEM!
RIGHTIO, OLD CHAP! IT SHALL BE DONE!

BUT SUDDENLY, AS THE INDIAN AND THE IRISH BOY REACHED THE EDGE OF A SMALL WOOD...
GET THEM!
GNNNG!

B-BY THE MISTS OF MOURNE, I– UUGH!
THUNK!
BLISTERING BANDICOOTS! WHAT'S GOIN' ON? COME ON, COBBERS. PILE IN!
OH, NO, YOU DON'T! FREEZE, ALL OF YOU! ANOTHER STEP AND YOU'LL BE DIGESTING BELLYFULS OF BUCKSHOT!
FRED, BACK ...THAT LENGTH OF RAIL. THESE MEN MUST HAVE LOOSENED IT. DELIBERATELY!
RIGHT FIRST TIME, KID! THERE'S A TRAIN DUE THROUGH CARRYING HALF A MILLION IN USED NOTES!

... AND HERE IT COMES! BANG ON SCHEDULE!
GUS! HELP ME GET MICK AND SADRA OFF THE LINE!
THE TRAIN DRIVER SUDDENLY SPOTTED THE DANGER, AND...
BROKEN RAIL AHEAD. BRAKE, MAN, FOR GLORY'S SAKE!
BUT IT WAS FAR TOO LATE!
GRAAH!
SCREECH!
KER RUNCH!
SECONDS LATER IT WAS ALL OVER, AND AN EERIE, DEATHLY SILENCE HUNG IN THE AIR...
RIGHT, MEN, YOU KNOW WHAT TO DO! BUST OPEN THE BULLION VANS AND GRAB THE SACKS OF MONEY. I'LL KEEP AN EYE ON THESE BRATS!
YOU BLACK-HEARTED DINGOES! WE'RE GOING TO SEE IF THE DRIVER AND HIS MATE ARE STILL ALIVE. COME ON, LADS!
ALTHOUGH DAZED AND SHOCKED, THE TWO MEN WERE NOT TOO BADLY HURT...
EASY DOES IT, COBBERS. JUST LIE STILL, DON'T TRY TO MOVE!
SURE, AND IT'S ENOUGH TO MAKE A MAN WEEP, CORPORAL! HERE WE ARE, FULLY ARMED WITH STENS ON A COMBAT TRAINING EXERCISE AND WE CAN'T DO A FLIPPIN' T'ING!
WORKING QUICKLY AND EFFICIENTLY, THE THIEVES COMPLETED THE ROBBERY WITHIN MINUTES. AND THEN...
BY THE SNOWS OF EVEREST, WHAT A DISASTER! THEY HAD A CAR WAITING. NOTHING CAN STOP THEM GETTING AWAY NOW!
DON'T BE TOO SURE, PEERAK. THIS AREA IS PRETTY REMOTE, AND THAT'S THE ONLY MAIN ROAD. IT SWINGS IN A BIG CURVE DOWN THE SIDE OF THE MOUNTAIN...

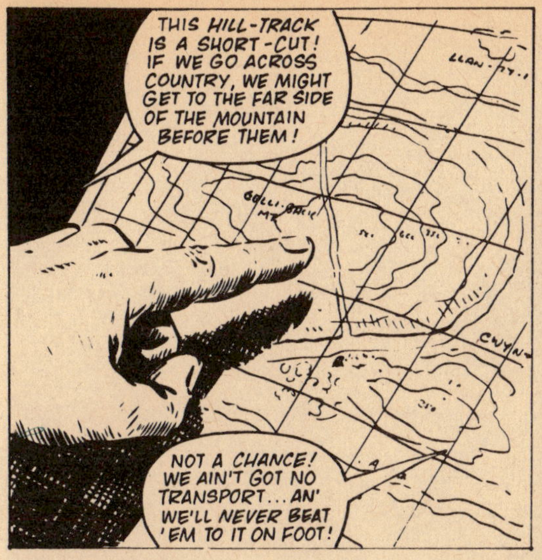
THIS HILL-TRACK IS A SHORT-CUT! IF WE GO ACROSS COUNTRY, WE MIGHT GET TO THE FAR SIDE OF THE MOUNTAIN BEFORE THEM!
NOT A CHANCE! WE AIN'T GOT NO TRANSPORT... AN' WE'LL NEVER BEAT 'EM TO IT ON FOOT!

USE YOUR INITIATIVE, YOU SAP-BRAINED BOOMER! WE'LL RIDE ACROSS THE MOUNTAIN. ON THOSE WELSH HILL-PONIES!
SWIPE ME WIV A WET SOCK! JEST MY BLINKIN' LUCK! THEM THINGS ARE HALF WILD!

BUT FRED'S MIND WAS MADE UP. AND SO...
NICE HORSE! COME ON, YOU 'ALF-BAKED BLIGHTER, COME CLOSER SO I CAN GET ON YOUR BLISTERIN' BACK!
HURRY IT UP, LEWIS! IF YOU CAN'T RAISE A GALLOP, YOU'LL JUST HAVE TO FOLLOW US IN YOUR OWN GOOD TIME!

TELLING THE INJURED RAILWAYMEN THEIR PLAN, FRED AND HIS CADETS RODE OFF... WHILE POOR DUFFY FELL FURTHER AND FURTHER BEHIND...
THEN, AN HOUR LATER, AFTER A HARD, DESPERATE RIDE...
GREAT SACKS O' HEATHER AN' HAGGIS! THERE IT IS - THE ROAD!
EMPTY, TOO! I RECKON WE'VE DONE IT, SPORTS! WE'VE GOT HERE FIRST!

OKAY, DISMOUNT AND DEPLOY YOURSELVES AMONG THOSE BOULDERS! WE'LL AMBUSH THE CAR AS IT COMES ROUND THE BEND. CHECK YOUR GUNS!

TENSELY THEY WAITED. FOR FIVE MINUTES ... TEN! AND THEN...
HERE THEY COME! AIM AT THE TYRES AND LET 'EM HAVE IT! FIRRRE!
SCREECH!

YAAAGH! IT'S THOSE KIDS! HOW THE BLAZES DID THEY GET AHEAD OF US?
RAT-A-TAT TAT!
ZING!
PWHEE!
BLAM!
TOO LATE TO WORRY ABOUT THAT NOW. DIVE INTO THE DITCH - WE'LL STAY HERE AND FIGHT IT OUT!

BUT CARNO'S CADETS WERE COOL AND HIGHLY-TRAINED. FIRING SHORT, SHARP BURSTS, THEY WORKED THEIR WAY CLOSER...
THAT'S THE STYLE, COBBERS! SLOW AND STEADY - WE'LL HAVE THE DINGOES OUTFLANKED IN A MINUTE!

BUT THEN, WITHOUT WARNING...
WHOOA, YOU STUPID NAG! STOP RUNNING, WE'RE 'ERE NOW!
HELP MA BOB, IT'S DUFFY! THE DAFT COCKNEY PUDDENHEID'S LET HIS PONY RUN AWA WI' HIM!

THAT BANK! OH ... NO!
YEEAGH!

GRAB THAT KID, HURRY! HE'S OUR PASS-PORT OUT OF HERE - WE'LL HOLD HIM AS A HOSTAGE!
RIGHT!

It's A Weird World

A glint of what seemed to be brass caught Malcolm Tricker's eye . . . but it turned out to be gold!

MALCOLM TRICKER w... erating his bulldozer o... site when he not... gleaming in the ex...y. Curious, he jumped down from his machine to find out what it was. He scraped away the earth with his hands and found five "odd-shaped bits of brass", as he called them.

Thinking they were old coffin handles or horse brasses, he took them home and washed them. Then Mr. Tricker realised they were not brass. He took his strange find to a museum expert, who told the bulldozer driver that he had made a very lucky strike.

The "bits of brass" were solid gold torques (necklaces) made about two thousand years ago.

Where There's MUCK There's MONEY

The great find was declared treasure trove and sent to the British Museum. Now, articles declared to be treasure trove become the property of the Crown, but if the owner has been honest and reported his find, the British Museum usually pays him the market value of the item.

Mr. Tricker unearthed the five torques in October 1968, and three months later the British Museum announced that the honest building worker was to be paid £45,000 for the "unique and outstanding examples of Early Iron Age craftsmanship."

People strike it rich in the most unusual and unexpected ways. Like George van Zyl, who recently made a surprising discovery under a rubbish dump! When he decided to move a rubbish pile left by previous owners of his land at Vredendal, South Africa, he found that the dump covered gravel containing a rich, untapped diamond vein. A fine example of the old saying "where there's muck there's money."

Mineral prospector John Johns spent years looking for a fortune in the desert of Western Australia. He found nothing. Then one day in 1969 his dog ran off after some rabbits. John went after the dog and found him chasing a rabbit round a rock.

"Suddenly I had a weird feeling about the place," the prospector said. "I took samples of the rock—and discovered one of the world's biggest nickel deposits."

And another animal, a donkey, discovered the richest silver-lead mine in the United States. It happened like this. Two prospectors named O'Rourke and Kellogg were travelling through the Idaho hills in 1885 when their pack-donkey wandered off and got lost.

If the donkey had not been carrying a lot of gear they wouldn't have bothered trailing it. But they did—and came upon a fabulous fortune. For when at last they found the donkey, the beast was standing on a great outcropping of silver-lead ore. This spot became the richest silver-lead mine in the United States, worth £20 million!

Ed Schieffelin was another American pioneer prospector who roamed the land hoping to strike

it rich. After trying his luck in Idaho, Utah, and Nevada, he drifted to Arizona in 1877, at that time the territory of hostile Apache Indians.

Finding a troop of soldiers about to leave for southern Arizona, Schieffelin joined them for protection. Soon, however, he decided to strike out on his own as he found the soldiers' progress not to his liking. The officer in charge bade him a pessimistic farewell: "Good luck, Ed, you'll need plenty of it. This is dangerous country . . . all you'll find out there is your tombstone!"

Ed Schieffelin was a stubborn man. He searched and searched and finally, in the San Pedro valley, he found silver. When he took a sample to the nearest assay office, the man there called him a "lucky cuss," and so Schieffelin decided to call his rich silver mine the "Lucky Cuss."

News of the silver strike spread and a town grew near the spot. Soon it needed a name and Schieffelin—who had a wry sense of humour—remembered the soldier's warning and called the town "Tombstone," a name that became famous in Wild West history.

A poor African shepherd boy struck it rich when he picked up a large bright stone near the Orange River in 1869. He carried the stone as a lucky charm, and lucky it proved to be. A Dutch farmer named van Niekerk recognised the stone charm as a diamond, an unpolished diamond of great size.

Van Niekerk offered the poor boy the entire livestock of his farm—500 sheep, ten oxen, and several horses—in trade for the diamond. The African boy thought van Niekerk must be crazy; for such a large number of animals represented a vast fortune in Africa at that time.

The shepherd boy accepted the offer and handed over the diamond. He was happy and rich beyond his dreams, and so was van Niekerk, for a few days later the farmer sold the gem in Hopetown for £10,000. And this famous diamond, known as the "Star of the South," is the one that started the great South African diamond rush in which many fortunes were made.

Nearly a hundred years later another boy, David Welham, discovered a fabulous treasure by accident. David, then aged four, was playing on a building site at Fishpool, near Newstead Abbey, Nottinghamshire, in 1966, when he found some old coins in the mud.

"This is dangerous country," said the cavalry officer. "All you'll find out there is your tombstone!"

David gave them to a workman, Mr. Bernard Beeton, who then searched further and picked up more than a hundred other coins. Mr. Beeton took them to the police, telling them that David had really found the coins. And it proved to be a remarkable discovery.

The coins were part of the fabulous "Fishpool Hoard"—Britain's most valuable find of historic coins—over a thousand gold pieces valued at £500,000. The 14th and 15th Century coins, many of them very rare, were declared treasure trove. The British Museum retained a number of the coins and the rest were auctioned for a vast amount of money, which was shared between the honest Mr. Beeton and the lucky David Welham.

Who knows, perhaps *you* too might strike it rich!

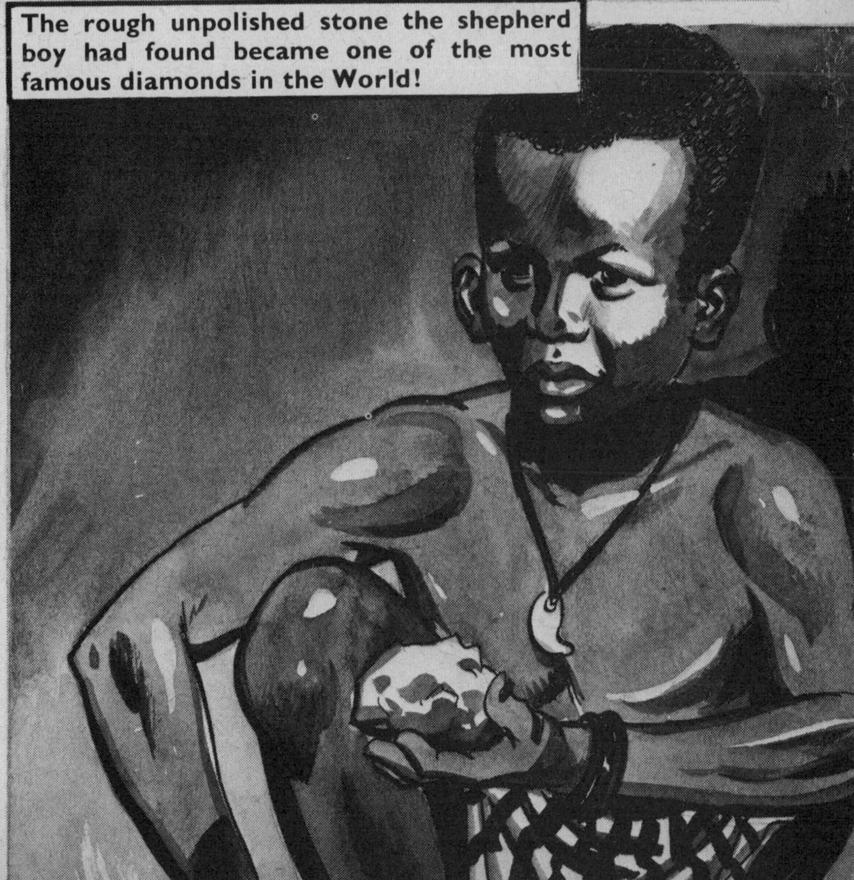

The rough unpolished stone the shepherd boy had found became one of the most famous diamonds in the World!

KESTER
KIDD

AN ARDUOUS LIFE AS A SHEPHERD BOY HAD GIVEN KESTER KIDD THE POWERS OF A SUPER-ATHLETE, SO BARNEY GRUMSHOTT DECIDED TO TRAIN HIM TO BE THE WORLD'S GREATEST ALL-ROUNDER. BUT BAD LUCK, PLUS THE DEVIOUS DESIGNS OF DOKTOR MUTTER, SPORTS DIRECTOR OF THE REPUBLIC OF SPOTZANIA, HAD PREVENTED KESTER ACHIEVING THE FAME HE DESERVED. AND SO THE PALS' TRAVELS BROUGHT THEM TO ITALY...
RACING RABBITS IS ALL RIGHT FOR TRAINING. BUT IF YOU'D CATCH ONE WE COULD HAVE SOMETHING TO EAT, KESTER!

AR, LIL' OL' RABBITS! OI COULDN'T DO THAT, BARNEY!
WE'VE BEEN WITHOUT GRUB FOR SO LONG IT DOESN'T MATTER, ANY-WAY. AT LEAST OUR LUCK CAN'T GET ANY WORSE!

BUT BARNEY DID NOT KNOW THEIR ARCH-ENEMY, DOKTOR MUTTER, WAS NEAR...
THAT BRITISH BRAT IS STILL THE ONLY ATHLETE WHO COULD PREVENT YOU BECOMING THE WORLD'S GREATEST, SUPERBO. BUT NOW I HAVE A NEW PLAN...THAT WILL PUT A STOP TO HIM ONCE AND FOR ALL!
HUUUUUH?

WE SHALL BREAK HIS SPIRIT! DESTROY HIS CONFIDENCE! AND THOSE PEASANTS HAVE AGREED TO HELP US. FOR CASH, OF COURSE!

FARMER BRUTO'S THREE SONS WERE IDENTICAL TRIPLETS...
IF YOUR THREE...ER...LADS KNOW WHAT TO DO I CONTACT THE BRITISH BRAT AT ONCE. WE SHALL RUN THE RACE THIS AFTERNOON.
OKAY! BUT YOU HAVE FORGOTTEN SOMETHING, SIGNOR!

YOU PROMISED US MONEY! ENOUGH FOR ME TO BUILD A NEW WATER-TOWER!
OF COURSE, MY FRIEND. HERE YOU ARE! HALF NOW... HALF WHEN THE BRITISH BRAT HAS LOST THE RACE!

WEARING ONE OF HIS MANY DEVIOUS DISGUISES, DOKTOR MUTTER WENT TO SEE KESTER AND BARNEY...
NEXT YEAR I INTEND TO HOLD A GREAT CROSS-COUNTRY MARATHON RACE HERE. BUT FIRST I MUST ENSURE THE COURSE IS SUITABLE. I HAVE ENGAGED A MAN TO TAKE PART IN A PRACTICE RACE...MAYBE YOUR FRIEND WOULD CARE TO COMPETE AGAINST HIM?

I WILL PAY THE WINNER ONE HUNDRED POUNDS IN ENGLISH MONEY..!
SAY NO MORE! KESTER WILL RACE!

AND SO, TWO HOURS LATER...
I WILL FOLLOW YOU OVER THE WHOLE TWENTY MILE COURSE IN MY PRIVATE PLANE. ON YOUR MARKS, GENTLEMEN... GET SET..!

CRAAAAACK!
GO!

WITHIN SECONDS THE BOY-WONDER ATHLETE WAS YARDS IN FRONT...
THE FINISHING LINE IS BACK AT THIS FARM. YOU WAIT HERE TO SEE WHO COMES IN FIRST!
OKAY! BUT I ALREADY KNOW WHO IT'LL BE!

DOKTOR MUTTER WAS CACKLING WITH EVIL GLEE...
THE BRITISH BRAT LEADS BY TWO MILES AT LEAST. BUT NOT FOR MUCH LONGER. HEE, HEEE! NOW I SHALL ACTIVATE THE FIRST OF MY MANY DEVIOUSLY-DEVISED, REMOTE-CONTROLLED HAZARDS!
YUUUUUH!

AND NEXT INSTANT...
YAAAAAAAHH!
RIGHT ON TARGET!.. TEE HEEEEE!
TRIP!

DANG OI! THERE BE A HOLE IN THE GROUND!
PERFECT! IT WILL TAKE THE BRITISH BRAT AT LEAST FIVE MINUTES TO GET OUT OF THAT PIT-TRAP. AND WHEN HE DOES...TEE HEE...HE'S IN FOR ANOTHER SHOCK!

THE SPOTZANIAN SPORTS DIRECTOR WAS RIGHT...
HECK! I THOUGHT THAT OTHER FELLER WAS MILES BEHIND!
THE POOR BRITISH FOOL DOES NOT REALISE THAT IS THE SECOND BRUTO BROTHER WHO WAS HIDING HERE AWAITING MY SIGNAL!

BUT KESTER WAS NOT TOO DISMAYED...
WHIIIIIIZ!
SAPRISTI! HE COMES LIKE THE WIND!

AND...
GOINK!
A THOUSAND CURSES! THE BOY HAS PASSED HIM! WHY WON'T THESE CURSED BRITISH GIVE UP MORE EASILY?

BUT NO MATTER! I HAVE ANOTHER TRAP PREPARED, AND THE THIRD BRUTO BROTHER WAITING TO TAKE OVER!
SUDDENLY, AS KESTER WAS WITHIN SIGHT OF THE FARMHOUSE FINISHING LINE...
FIRST A CONCEALED TAPE-RECORDER IMITATES THE SOUND OF A SHEEP IN DISTRESS..!
BAAAAAA!
DANG OI! OI MUST GO AND SEE WHAT AILS THAT POOR CRITTER!
OI BE MILES AHEAD OF THE OTHER FELLER AGAIN. AND THAT THERE POOR CRITTER DOES SOUND IN MORTAL TROUBLE!
BAAAAAAAA!
BAAAAAIIIIII!
THEN DOKTOR MUTTER JABBED ANOTHER CONTROL BUTTON...
COO! 'TIS A BIG OWD RAM! AN' HE DO LOOK PROPER ANGRY, LOIKE!
BWAAAAAAAARRR!
NOW I RELEASE THAT VICIOUS ANIMAL I HIRED FROM BRUTO! TEE HEE...AT THIS WE MUST TAKE A CLOSER LOOK!
AS THE MASSIVE RAM CHARGED TOWARDS HIM...
HEE HEE...HE'S JUST STANDING THERE! I MUST SEE THIS CLOSER STILL!
OI DON'T WANT TO RUN AWAY FROM HIM! MIGHT HURT HIS FEELIN'S LOIKE!
THRUM! THRUM! THRUM!
THEN...
OI DIDN'T THINK ABOUT THAT WALL THERE!
A THOUSAND CURSES! IT MISSED HIM!
BAAAAAAA!

BUT THE HURTLING WALL-STONES DIDN'T MISS DOKTOR MUTTER'S PLANE...
THUNK!
SPLUTTER!
OH NO!
BANG!
RIIIP!
DANG OI!
CRAASH!

BALE OUT! GRAB A PARACHUTE! IT'S GOING TO CRASH!

ZOOOOMM-
MAMA MIA...!
WE'RE TOO LOW! OUR PARACHUTES WON'T OPEN IN TIME!

AN OOZING MUD-POND BROKE THE SPOTZANIANS' FALL...
GROOOOOOOOHH!
CRAAAASH!
CREEEAK!..CRAAAACK!

SECONDS LATER...
DANG OI! HE WENT AND PASSED ME AGAIN!

I...I CANNOT CROSS THIS!
WIIIIIIIIIIIZ!
THIS BE A ROIGHT FUNNY RACE, THIS BE! BUT OI PROMISED BARNEY I'D WIN IT FOR HIM!

SO OI RECKON I'D BETTER DO IT, LOIKE!
YOU'RE IN FIRST, KESTER! WE'VE WON!
MY TOWER! GRAAAAAAAHH! YOU HAVE DESTROYED IT!

YOU PAY ME FOR NEW TOWER, AND YOU PAY HIM, TOO!
Y-Y-Y-YES! OF COURSE! I...I'LL PAY...GRUUUUUH!

THANK 'EE FOR THE RACE, MISTER! OI HOPE IT GO REAL ROIGHT FOR 'EE NEXT YEAR!
BAAAAAH!

FORTUNATELY FOR MUTTER AND SUPERBO, BARNEY AND KESTER HAD NO MORE NEED FOR THEIR TENT...
ALL MY MONEY GONE! NOT EVEN A DECENT ROOF OVER OUR HEADS!
GLOIIIINK!

AND TO MAKE IT WORSE, WE FAILED! AND...AND I HAVE TO REPORT TO OUR PRESIDENT THAT WE'VE CRASHED ANOTHER PLANE!..

ONCE AGAIN BARNEY GRUMSHOTT AND KESTER KIDD, THE WONDER ATHLETE, WERE ON THE LONG ROAD TO FAME ...
THIS BE A ROIGHT GOOD TRAINING PLAN, BARNEY.
DON'T GO TOO FAST, KESTER! DON'T GO TEARING OFF AHEAD. WE DON'T WANT TO LOSE EACH OTHER...'COS WE'VE GOT RECORDS TO BREAK!
THE END!

RED FOX and the BAD BOYS

ALL readers of "The Kids of Stalag 41" enjoy the antics of Winston and his lads when they get up to their hilarious attempts to escape from the dopey Kolonel Schtink's prison camp—but here are a few accounts of *real-life* escape attempts from wartime prisons!

They called Mike Sinclair the "Red Fox". This British army officer was the star performer of one of the most amazing escape attempts from Colditz Castle, the maximum security prisoner of war camp in the heart of Germany.

Colditz Castle (Oflag IVC) was a special "escape-proof" camp for allied officers during the Second World War. Only the "bad boys" —the incurable escapers from other camps—were sent to Colditz, a formidable high-walled 16th Century castle situated on the top of a hill.

It was indeed a tough place to get away from, but it wasn't escape-proof as the Germans claimed. Thirty "home runs" were made by prisoners; a "home run" was a successful escape that got you back to England.

The British officers at Colditz organised a highly-efficient escapers' club, using the collective and varied talents of many brilliant men to devise ingenious plans, produce false identity papers, make German uniforms, and fashion special tools.

Mike Sinclair's astonishing plan was to impersonate the sergeant of the guard, a portly German known to the prisoners as "Franz Josef" because of his enormous moustache and resemblance to Franz Josef, the former Emperor of Austria. Sinclair, made up as the sergeant, would relieve the guard, obtain the keys to the main gate, and walk to freedom with a large group of prisoners!

The Red Fox, who spoke fluent German, spent three months studying Franz Josef; the way he walked and talked. The escape club had to produce three perfect German uniforms—for Sinclair and two phoney guards—complete with wooden rifles and bayonet scabbards. Came the night of the big show and Sinclair, padded round the middle and with a huge moustache covering half his face, marched out with his two German-uniformed mates to try the great bluff.

Sinclair replaced one genuine sentry and then approached the guard at the gate. He demanded the keys of the gate, which the sentry gave him . . . but then things began to go wrong. The real Franz Josef suddenly appeared on the scene and came face to face with his other self!

The Red Fox didn't panic. He had shot his bolt but he was going to bluff it out to the bitter end. The real Franz Josef, having recovered from the shock, shouted orders to the guards. Sinclair snapped out counter-commands. The German soldiers stared at the two sergeants, obeying one and then the other, until the crazy scene dissolved into confusion. Then a shot rang out and Mike Sinclair fell wounded. The show was over.

The Colditz escape club developed other plans. Some worked, some didn't. One simple idea that proved stunningly successful was carried out by an athletic Frenchman, Lieutenant Lebrun. At various times the prisoners were taken out of the castle to play football, or exercise, in a park; the prisoners played in a compound surrounded by wire and guards armed with rifles.

Lebrun, dressed in shorts and gym shoes, was in the habit of doing team exercises with a group of Frenchmen, such as leapfrogging each other. The guards were used to seeing this kind of activity. One day a Frenchman stood close to the wire fence and, forming a stirrup with his hands into which Lebrun placed a foot, he catapulted the agile lieutenant upwards and over the nine-foot fence!

By the time the guards recovered their wits and fired a few shots, the leaping Lebrun was clear away. He was never recaptured.

Wherever British prisoners were held in German camps there

Lebrun took the German guards by surprise . . . his friend catapulted him over the barbed wire fence—to freedom!

was always an escaping club. When Captain Douglas of a Highland regiment decided to leave Stalag XXI with the garbage, the club agreed to help him. The prison camp consisted of a number of stone buildings surrounded by barbed wire, a deep moat, and a second fence of barbed wire.

The only exit was a pair of heavily-guarded steel gates leading on to a drawbridge across the moat. At eight o'clock every morning the gates opened and the drawbridge was lowered for the truck carrying the garbage, which was tipped beyond the outer ring of barbed wire. Captain Douglas decided to break out of the camp by hiding under the load of rubbish.

Members of the escape club tied up a sack with Douglas inside and put him into one of the wooden barrels that stood in a row, filled with garbage, waiting to be picked up by the truck in the morning.

Next morning, Douglas was emptied into the truck with the rubbish. The stink, as you can imagine, was awful. At the gate, two guards poked the load of refuse with long poles and were satisfied that nobody was hidden there. And so Douglas was tipped into the rubbish dump. Later, he cut himself out of the sack and went on to make a home run.

Now let us return to Colditz and the most ingenious escape plan of all time. The amazing idea was to build a glider in a secret workshop with the clear intention of flying it out of the camp. It would carry two men and be launched from one of the castle's tall roofs.

To begin with, a false wall was built in a little-used attic so that a casual glance by a guard would not immediately reveal that half the area had disappeared. Plans for a glider with a 33ft wingspan were drawn, and materials—mainly wood and canvas—were smuggled into the secret workshop. Nearly a year was spent on the fantastic project.

At last the glider was finished. It had a wide skid under the front of the fuselage to assist with the launching. The skin of the aircraft was made from prison sleeping bags of blue and white checked cotton. Of course, no test flight could be made. Whether it flew or not would only be found out on the day it was launched to freedom.

The launching method was also ingenious. The glider was to be pulled through a hole to the peak of the roof. A bathtub filled with set cement was fixed to the front of the glider by a cable, which could be released by the pilot; the heavy bathtub would slide down the roof and jerk the glider into the air with considerable force. It sounded crazy, but would it work? Well, the glider was never put to the test.

The end of the war was near and the allies liberated Colditz just before the glider was due to be used. Would it have flown? After the war the engineering plans of the Colditz glider were examined by the experts of the British aircraft firm of de Havilland, and they were in no doubt that the glider would have flown successfully.

It was an ingenious escape plan—the idea was to launch a glider from the castle roof. But there would be no chance to make a test flight!

VON HOFFMAN'S
INVASION

DR. VON HOFFMAN, AN EVIL SCIENTIFIC GENIUS, HAD INVENTED AN AMAZING GAS WHICH COULD ENLARGE ALL CREATURES AND INSECTS, AND HE WAS USING IT TO DESTROY ANYTHING WHICH WAS A SYMBOL OF PRIDE AND TRIUMPH TO GREAT BRITAIN. SUCH A SYMBOL OF BRITANNIA'S GREATNESS WAS THE "EMPIRE QUEEN", A REVOLUTIONARY NEW HOVER-SHIP, WHICH WAS ABOUT TO BE LAUNCHED FROM THE CHANNEL PORT OF WESTHAMPTON!
AND I NAME THIS VESSEL ...THE "EMPIRE QUEEN"! MAY GOOD FORTUNE FOLLOW HER, AND ALL WHO SAIL IN HER!
WELL SAID, LADY CRUMSHAW!
HURRAAAW! SHE'S AWAY..!
TINKLE!
CRASH

AS THE MAGNIFICENT CRAFT SLID SEAWARDS ON A WHINING CUSHION OF AIR...
WHAT A GLORIOUS SIGHT! THE "QUEEN" CAN CARRY NEARLY 500 PEOPLE, AND COST OVER £20,000,000 TO BUILD!
IT WOULD BE A DISASTER FOR ALL TRUE ENGLISHMEN, IF THAT FIEND, VON HOFFMAN, MANAGED TO DESTROY HER!
WHRREEEEEEEEE

HE WON'T GET THE CHANCE, THIS TIME! HERE COME THE WARSHIPS WHICH ARE GOING TO ESCORT THE "QUEEN" ACROSS THE CHANNEL ON HER MAIDEN VOYAGE!
HURRAAAAY! UP THE NAVY..!

ON BOARD THE FLAGSHIP OF THE ESCORT-FLOTILLA...
THIS IS MR. JEFF HUNTER, COMMANDER!
OF COURSE! THE MAN WHO, MORE THAN ANYONE ELSE, IS RESPONSIBLE FOR THWARTING MANY OF VON HOFFMAN'S NEFARIOUS SCHEMES!
THANK YOU, SIR! BUT YOU'RE FORGETTING BARRY AND JOEY DRAKE..!

THE TOUGH GAME-WARDEN POINTED TO THE TWO BOYS, WHO HAD FIRST DISCOVERED THE MENACE OF VON HOFFMAN...
IT WAS THESE TWO LADS WHO STUMBLED ON THE INSECTICIDE...X2F04... WHICH HAS THE POWER TO SHRINK VON HOFFMAN'S GIANTS! AS YOU CAN SEE, THEY ARE MIXING THE FORMULA WITH ORDINARY SEA-WATER..!

ONCE WE'VE GOT THE RIGHT BLEND, THE WATER CAN BE PUMPED INTO THAT WATER-CANNON, AND BLASTED OUT OVER A WIDE AREA!
SO YOU'RE EXPECTING AN ATTACK FROM THE AIR? GIANT SEA-BIRDS, AND THE LIKE?

IT'S THE ONLY WAY THAT VON HOFFMAN COULD ATTACK US, SIR! APART FROM THE ODD SHARK, I CAN'T THINK OF ANY CREATURES IN THE CHANNEL WHICH ARE DEADLY ENOUGH TO HARM THE "QUEEN"... EVEN IF HOFFMAN COULD GET CLOSE ENOUGH TO USE HIS GAS ON THEM! AND THAT'S VIRTUALLY IMPOSSIBLE!

BUT, AT THAT VERY MOMENT, ON THE SEA-FRONT OF WESTHAMPTON...
RAAAEEECH!
BRRMMBLE!
AAAAAAH! RUN! IT'S COMING THIS WAY!
I... D-DON'T BELIEVE IT..!

A GIANT ELEPHANT! BUT WHERE DID IT COME FROM?
IT MUST BE THE ONE THAT WAS STOLEN FROM THAT SAFARI PARK, THE OTHER NIGHT..!
KRUNCH!

VON HOFFMAN MUST HAVE ENLARGED IT! AND-LOOK! THERE HE IS... SITTING ON THE ELEPHANT'S BACK!
ON, MY BEAUTY! DON'T EVEN STOP AT THE TRAFFIC-LIGHTS! YA! HA! HEEEEE!

CROWDS SCATTERED IN TERROR, AS THE EVIL MASTER-SCIENTIST BROUGHT HIS COLOSSAL STEED TO A HALT!
BAWWWEEEEEEE!
WESTHAMPTON
AQUARIUM
AND HERE WE ARE... THE "WESTHAMPTON AQUARIUM". INSIDE IT ARE ALL THE CREATURES THAT I NEED TO DESTROY THE "EMPIRE QUEEN"!

SO START TEARING OFF THE ROOF, GREAT ONE! CAREFULLY, NOW! WE DO NOT WISH TO DAMAGE ZE TANKS..!
RRRRNNNNNGH!

SOON...
NOW LET ME SEE..! AH, YES! ZAIR ISS ONE OF THE SPECIMENS I AM LOOKING FOR! DIP YOUR TRUNK INTO THE LARGEST TANK, MY BEAUTY..!

REACTING TO THE VERY SOUND OF VON HOFFMAN'S VOICE, THE COLOSSAL ELEPHANT OBEYED!
ONCE YOU HAF DRAINED THAT TANK, EMPTY THE ONE ON YOUR RIGHT! AND THEN THE FOURTH ONE ALONG..!
BABY SWORD FISH
SSSSSUUUUFFFFF!

THE STRANGE TASK WAS SOON COMPLETED!
UND NOW... AWAY TO THE HARBOUR! WHERE ANOTHER MIRACULOUS PRODUCT OF MY INVENTIVE BRAIN AWAITS US..!
TEAS ICES

...A HIGH POWERED MOTOR-CRUISER! COMPLETE WIZ ITS OWN, BUILT-IN FISH-TANK! START SQUIRTING, GREAT ONE!

AS SOON AS YOU HAF EMPTIED YOUR TRUNK - LIFT ME DOWN! I MUST MAKE SURE THAT THE SPECIMENS HAF NOT SUFFERED FROM THEIR ORDEAL!
FROOOOOSH!

ONCE AGAIN, THE MIGHTY ELEPHANT OBEYED! AND HAVING CLAMBERED ABOARD THE BOAT, VON HOFFMAN PEERED ANXIOUSLY INTO THE TANK...
YES...HEE, HEE! ALL ALIVE UND KICKINK! THE THREE WEAPONS THAT THOSE FOOLS OUT THERE WILL NOT BE EXPECTING ME TO USE!

WITH A LAST, GLEEFUL CRY TO HIS FORMER ALLY, VON HOFFMAN WENT SPEEDING ON HIS ERRAND OF DESTRUCTION!
BAWWWHEEEEEEF!
FAREWELL, GREAT ONE! SOON, YOU WILL RETURN TO NORMAL SIZE! IN THE MEANTIME, CONTINUE THE HAVOC THAT WE STARTED! DO NOT GIVE ZEM TIME TO RAISE THE ALARM!

WELL OUT INTO THE CHANNEL, VON HOFFMAN CUT HIS ENGINES, AND WENT SWIFTLY TO WORK...
FIRST... A COUPLE OF MY ENLARGING GAS PILLS, DROPPED INTO ZE TANK..!
SSSSSSS!

UND NOW TO DUMP THE CONTENTS OF THE TANK OVERBOARD— BEFORE ZE GAS TAKES EFFECT..!
SWOOOSH!

A SPLIT-SECOND AFTER THE TANK HAD BEEN EMPTIED...
SPLUNNGE!
THE GAS IS TAKING EFFECT..! THE WORLD IS ABOUT TO WITNESS THREE MORE EXAMPLES OF MY WIZARDRY..!

PLOP!
CRACKLE!
...AN OCTOPUS ...A SWORD-FISH... UND AN ELECTRIC EEL! ALL DEDICATED TO THE DESTRUCTION OF THE "EMPIRE QUEEN"! AHEEEEEEE!
BLUUURP!

FIVE MINUTES LATER, TO THE UTTER AMAZEMENT OF THE MEN ABOARD ONE OF THE ESCORTING FRIGATES...
S-STONE ME! ACTION-STATIONS! SWORD-FISH ON THE PORT BEAM!
IT'S NEARLY HALF AS BIG AS THE SHIP... COMING STRAIGHT AT US!

EVERY GUN THAT COULD BE BROUGHT TO BEAR OPENED UP ON THE ONRUSHING MONSTER...
THIS MUST BE VON HOFFMAN'S WORK! HE'S TRYING TO BLAST HIS WAY THROUGH TO THE 'QUEEN'!
WE'VE HIT IT A HUNDRED TIMES! BUT IT'S STILL COMING..!

ALTHOUGH MORTALLY WOUNDED, THE HUGE FISH LUNGED ON... AND STRUCK THE SHIP WITH THE FORCE OF A GIANT STEEL-TIPPED ARROW!
AAAAAGH! ITS SWORD'S GONE CLEAN THROUGH THE HULL..!
SCRUUUNCH!

WE'RE HOLED BELOW THE WATER-LINE.... GOING DOWN FAST!
ABANDON SHIP!

ABOARD THE FLAGSHIP, THE DRAKES, AND JEFF HUNTER, WERE HELPLESS WITNESSES OF THE AMAZING TRAGEDY...
GOSH, WHERE ON EARTH DID OLD VON HOFFMAN GET HIS HANDS ON THAT SWORD-FISH? HE'S ATTACKED IN A WAY THAT WE LEAST EXPECTED, JEFF!
BUT HE WON'T GET MUCH FARTHER, BARRY! THERE GOES THE "INVINCIBLE" TO BLAST HIS BOAT OUT OF THE WATER!

BUT, BEFORE A SINGLE SHOT COULD BE FIRED...
WH-WHAT'S THAT? BREAKING THE SURFACE ASTERN OF US..?
IT...L-LOOKS LIKE A... GIANT ELECTRIC EEL!

IT WAS! VON HOFFMAN'S SECOND MONSTER STRUCK WITH VICIOUS SPEED...
AAAAAHHHHH!

A FEW MOMENTS LATER...
SIGNAL FROM "INVINCIBLE", SIR! MOST OF THE CREW STUNNED BY A COLOSSAL ELECTRIC SHOCK! STEERING GEAR DAMAGED! SHE ...SHE'S OUT OF CONTROL, SIR!
GREAT SCOTT! THIS MEANS THAT WE'RE ALL THAT STANDS BETWEEN THE "QUEEN" AND THAT MADMAN NOW!

BUT VON HOFFMAN WAS ABOUT TO SEND HIS THIRD ALLY TO THE ATTACK!
GO, MY BEAUTY! THAT ACCURSED BRITISH MASTERPIECE IS AT YOUR MERCY! DRAG HER INTO THE DEPTHS..!

THE COLOSSAL OCTOPUS MOVED WITH FANTASTIC SPEED! AND, SECONDS LATER...
SPLOOOM!
YEEEAAAAH! CUT THE ENGINES! FULL SPEED ASTERN..!

BUT IT WAS TOO LATE!
EEEEEEEEEGH!
THE "QUEEN'S" TRAPPED IN THOSE MONSTROUS TENTACLES! AND WE DARE NOT OPEN FIRE, WITH ALL THOSE PASSENGERS ABOARD!
THE FLAGSHIP'S HELICOPTER, SIR! IT'S THEIR ONLY HOPE NOW..!

LEAVING NOTHING TO CHANCE, JEFF HUNTER HAD ALREADY ERECTED A WEIRD APPARATUS ABOARD THE 'COPTER!
IT'S A SORT OF GIANT CROSS-BOW, SIR....FIRING HUGE, HYPODERMIC DARTS! I'VE USED IT AGAINST VON HOFFMAN'S MONSTERS BEFORE!
THEN LET'S HOPE IT WORKS! YOU'RE CLEARED FOR TAKE-OFF..!

THAKKA! THAKKA!
HERE WE GO, LADS! START FILLING THE WAR-HEAD OF ONE OF THE DARTS WITH INSECTICIDE, BARRY!
OKAY, JEFF..!

EEEEEAAAAARGH!
WE'LL ONLY HAVE TIME FOR ONE SHOT! A COUPLE MORE HEAVES FROM THAT OCTOPUS, AND THE "EMPIRE QUEEN" IS FINISHED!

I'M ALL SET, JEFF! DART LOADED, AND READY TO FIRE!
OKAY! I'LL TAKE HER DOWN AS CLOSE AS I DARE! AND FOR PETE'S SAKE- DON'T MISS!

NOW..... LET HER GO!
THWAAANG!

BARRY'S SHOT WAS RIGHT ON TARGET! WITH A DULL THUD, THE DART BURIED ITSELF IN THE MONSTER'S SLITHERY BULK...
BULLS-EYE! WE'LL HAVE TO WAIT A FEW SECONDS FOR THE INSECTICIDE TO ENTER ITS BLOOD-STREAM...!
WHOOOOMP!

AND THERE SHE GOES! THE MONSTER'S SHRINKING!
YIPPEEEEE, WE'VE DONE IT! WE'VE SAVED THE "EMPIRE QUEEN"!
WHEEEOOOOOM!

AND NOW FOR VON HOFFMAN! A COUPLE OF DEPTH-CHARGES IN HIS LAP, AND BRITAIN WILL BE RID OF HIS MENACE FOR EVER!
DONNER UND BLITZEN! N-NO..!

BUT THE EVIL MASTER-SCIENTIST HAD COME PREPARED FOR SUCH AN EMERGENCY...
IT VOS INDEED FORTUNATE THAT I TOOK THE PRECAUTION OF BRINGING YOU ALONG, MR. SEAGULL..!
STUUUF!
STUUUF!

ONCE AGAIN, THE AMAZING ENLARGING-GAS TOOK INSTANT EFFECT...
SHOOOOM!
HA-HEEEEEEE! AWAY WITH ME, MY FANTASTIC FEATHERED FRIEND! CARRY ME BEYOND THE REACH OF THAT PUNY HELICOPTER..!
KRAAAK!

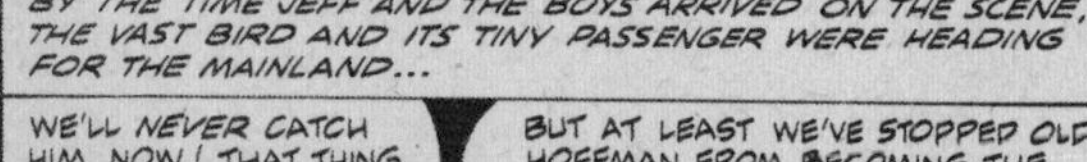
BY THE TIME JEFF AND ITS THE BOYS ARRIVED ON THE SCENE, THE VAST BIRD AND ITS TINY PASSENGER WERE HEADING FOR THE MAINLAND...

WE'LL NEVER CATCH HIM NOW! THAT THING IS SO BIG, IT MUST BE FLYING AT OVER A HUNDRED MILES PER HOUR!
BUT AT LEAST WE'VE STOPPED OLD HOFFMAN FROM BECOMING THE GREATEST PIRATE EVER KNOWN! I'LL BET HE AIN'T HALF MAD, BARRY..!

VOEY DRAKE WAS RIGHT! A LAST INFURIATED CRY DRIFTED BACK ACROSS THE WATER...
FOILED IN MY MOMENT OF GLORY....BY HUNTER AND THOSE ACCURSED BRATS! BUT VON HOFFMAN LIVES TO FIGHT ON! SOMEHOW, SOMEWHERE, I SHALL STRIKE AGAIN! DOWN WITH GREAT BRITAIN!
THE END.

JEST A MINUTE!

GALLIPOLI PROVED THEM A REGIMENT OF HEROES!
The MINDEN BOYS
EGYPT
LANCASHIRE THE FUSILIERS
"SIX V.C.s BEFORE BREAKFAST"! THAT IS THE PROUD BOAST OF THIS NORTH COUNTRY REGIMENT. ON 25th APRIL, 1915, THE 1st BATTALION, LANCASHIRE FUSILIERS LANDED FROM OPEN BOATS ON "W" BEACH AT GALLIPOLI...
THROUGH WITHERING FIRE FROM TURKISH MACHINE GUNS, THROUGH A MAZE OF BARBED WIRE, THE TOUGH FUSILIERS PRESSED ON. SIX OF THEM WERE TO GAIN THE CROSS FOR VALOUR FOR THIS MORNING'S WORK... AND "W" BEACH WAS TO BE RENAMED "LANCASHIRE LANDING"...

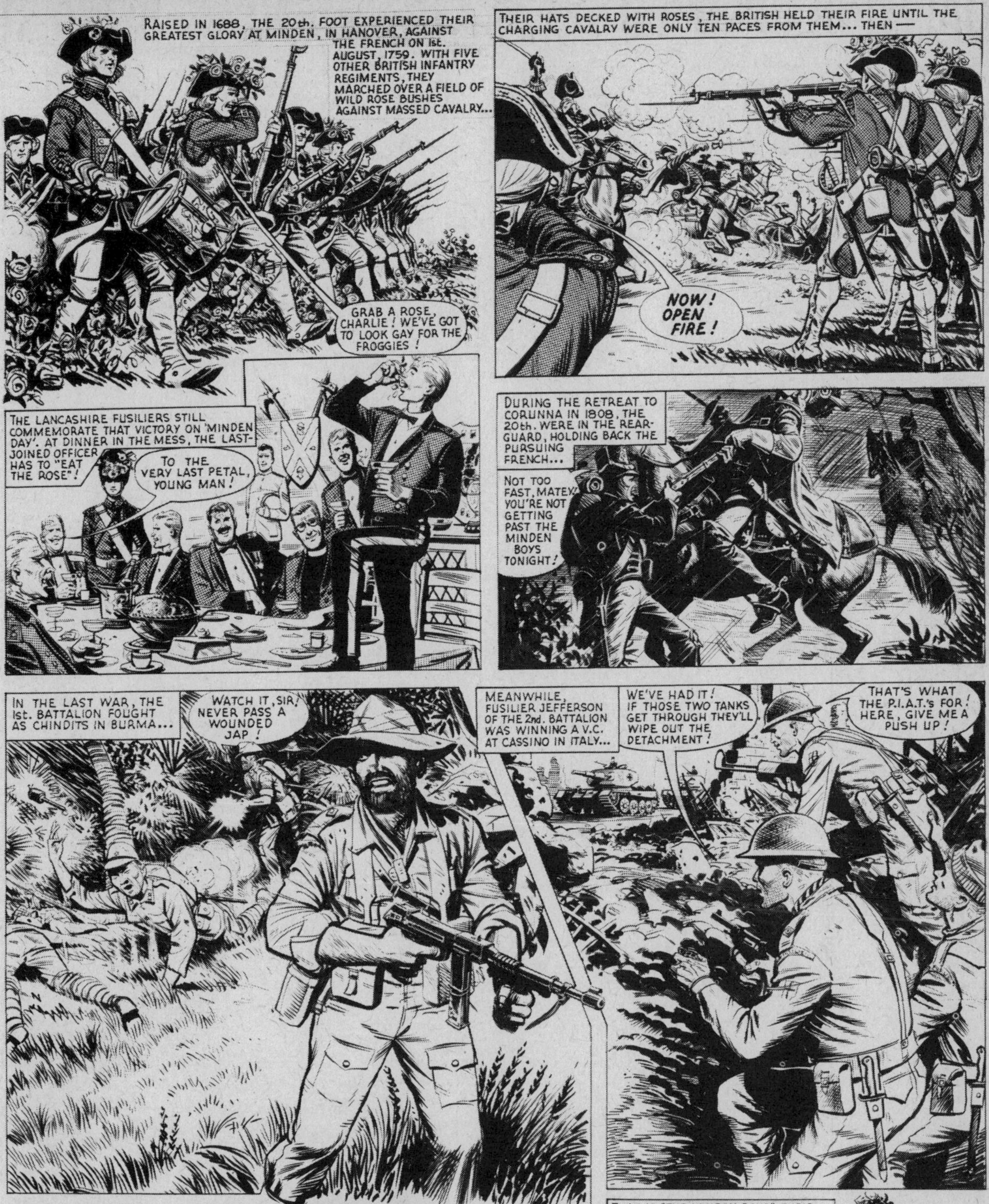

IN THE LAST WAR, THE 1st. BATTALION FOUGHT AS CHINDITS IN BURMA...

WATCH IT, SIR! NEVER PASS A WOUNDED JAP!

MEANWHILE, FUSILIER JEFFERSON OF THE 2nd. BATTALION WAS WINNING A V.C. AT CASSINO IN ITALY...

WE'VE HAD IT! IF THOSE TWO TANKS GET THROUGH THEY'LL WIPE OUT THE DETACHMENT!

THAT'S WHAT THE P.I.A.T.'s FOR! HERE, GIVE ME A PUSH UP!

THAT'S BREWED YOU UP, JERRY! NOW FOR THE NEXT ONE!

THAT IS "THE MINDEN BOYS", THEIR FAVOURITE NICKNAME. A ROSE IN THEIR HATS OR A BAZOOKA IN THEIR FISTS, THE FIGHTING TWENTIETH, NOW SERVING IN THE FUSILIER BRIGADE, MARCH ON! READY FOR ANYTHING ... ANYWHERE!

THE SLUDGEMOUTH SLOGGERS
GENERAL STORES
GARAGE
ANTIQUES
BINGO
BUTCHER
DRY CLEANERS
WET
BUILDER
ODEON
GROCER
LAUNDRY

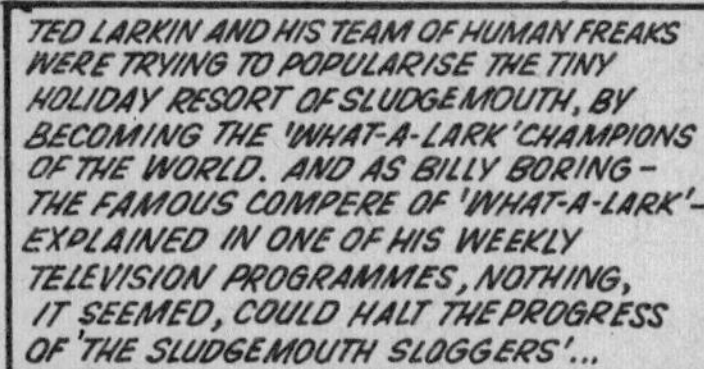
TED LARKIN AND HIS TEAM OF HUMAN FREAKS WERE TRYING TO POPULARISE THE TINY HOLIDAY RESORT OF SLUDGEMOUTH, BY BECOMING THE 'WHAT-A-LARK' CHAMPIONS OF THE WORLD. AND AS BILLY BORING - THE FAMOUS COMPERE OF 'WHAT-A-LARK' - EXPLAINED IN ONE OF HIS WEEKLY TELEVISION PROGRAMMES, NOTHING, IT SEEMED, COULD HALT THE PROGRESS OF 'THE SLUDGEMOUTH SLOGGERS'...

AND HERE WE SEE THE SLOGGERS WITH THEIR LATEST TROPHY, VIEWERS... WON AT THE EXPENSE OF BRIGHTSEA! A TRIUMPH MADE POSSIBLE BY THE ONE THING THAT MAKES SLUDGEMOUTH DIFFERENT FROM ALL THE OTHER RESORTS...

MILLIONS OF 'WHAT-A-LARK' FANS FINISHED BILLY'S SENTENCE...
IT'S ALWAYS RAINING IN SLUDGEMOUTH!
HEE, HEE! HAAAR! YOU'VE GOT IT, FOLKS!
PELTING, IN FACT!

THANKS TO ITS ROTTEN WEATHER, THERE'S MORE 'SLUDGE' IN SLUDGEMOUTH, THAN SAND! AS BRIGHTSEA DISCOVERED TO THEIR COST, IN THE FIVE-LEGGED OBSTACLE RACE!
BRIGHTSEA ARE LEADING, WITH JUST THE BARREL-JUMP TO COME! IF THEY CAN CLEAR IT SAFELY, THEY'RE HOME AND DRY!

"THE TROUBLE WITH SLUDGEMOUTH IS IT'S NEVER DRY! HA, HA! A SHARP SHOWER OF RAIN HAS CHURNED MOST OF THE COURSE INTO A QUAGMIRE..."
THWUUUUMP!
VEEAAAGH!
BRIGHTSEA HAVE SKIDDED IN THE MUD! THEY'VE GONE INTO THE BARRELS INSTEAD OF OVER 'EM!

"BUT NOT THE SLOGGERS, FOLKS! KNOWN ONLY TO THEM, A NARROW PATHWAY OF FIRM GROUND RAN STRAIGHT UP THE MIDDLE OF THE COURSE..."
HEAD FOR THE BARRELS SIDE-ON, LADS! KEEP TO THE HIDDEN CAUSEWAY!

SO, OVER THE BARRELS THEY SOARED... AND ON TO FINAL VICTORY...
YA-HAAAY! SLOG IT TO 'EM, SLUDGEMOUTH!

BUT NOW SLUDGEMOUTH MAY BE IN FOR A TASTE OF ITS OWN MEDICINE! THIS PROGRAMME IS COMING FROM CHILBAY... THE SLOGGERS' OPPONENTS IN THE FINAL OF THE WESTERN REGION 'WHAT-A-LARK' CHALLENGE CUP...
...AND WHEN I SAY THAT CHILBAY ARE ALSO DIFFICULT TO BEAT ON THEIR HOME TERRITORY, THAT'S PUTTING IT MILDLY! WATCH WHAT HAPPENS WHEN I OPEN THIS DOOR!
OOOGH! SEE WHAT I MEAN, VIEWERS? THIS IS JUST A SAMPLE OF...
WHEEEEOOOOOOOSH!
FLOMMP!
...THE DREADED WIND OF CHILBAY! WINTER AND SUMMER, IT'S ALWAYS BLOWING! THE LOCALS HAVE LEARNED TO LIVE WITH IT...
...BUT WHAT WILL THE SLOGGERS MAKE OF IT? CAN THEY OVERCOME THIS FIENDISH FREAK OF NATURE, AND PUT THE WIND UP CHILBAY? YA, HA, HEEEE!
EVEN AS BILLY BORING WAS SPEAKING, STRANGE EVENTS WERE TAKING PLACE IN FAR-OFF SLUDGEMOUTH...
KEEP GOING, SLOGGERS! KEEP THE GIANT EGG HEAD-ON INTO THE WIND!
EGAD! GASP...
THE WEIRD TRAINING SESSION WAS BEING HELD AT A LOCAL AIRFRAME-TESTING ESTABLISHMENT...
NOW START... TURNING THE OTHER WAY! SHIELD THE EGG WITH YOUR BODIES!
OOO-AAR! WE'S GETTIN' THE KNACKY-DOODLE OF THIS A TREAT, HEE, HEE!

IN PERFECT RHYTHM, THE SLOGGERS SWUNG WITH THE GALE...
... AND THERE WE ARE – THROUGH THE FINISHING TAPE BACKWARDS! NICE GOING, LADS!
THE GIANT EGG DIDN'T EVEN WOBBLE!
I THINK WE'VE GOT THE HANG OF IT NOW! THANKS FOR THE LOAN OF YOUR WIND-TUNNEL, BERT!
GOOD LUCK AT CHILBAY SLOGGERS!
YOU'RE WELCOME, TED! IT WAS WORKING AT FULL-BLAST, SO YOU SHOULD BE READY FOR ANYTHING NOW!
WAH-HAAAY!
GOOD IDEA, TED... USING THE WIND-TUNNEL FOR TRAINING!
CHILBAY WON'T HAVE AN ADVANTAGE OVER US NOW! THE BEST TEAM WILL WIN... AND I RECKON THAT'S US!
BUT AT THAT VERY MOMENT, SOMEWHERE ON CHILBAY'S WIND-LASHED SEA-FRONT...
... AS I SAID, MR. MAYOR! SLUDGEMOUTH WILL ALMOST CERTAINLY BE TAKING STEPS TO COUNTERACT THE EFFECT OF THE CHILBAY WIND!
BUT YOU'VE COME UP WITH A COUNTER COUNTER-PLAN, EH, REG? AND WHAT'S THAT?
REG WANGLER, THE MANAGER OF THE CHILBAY TEAM, POINTED TO A WEIRD FORMATION OF ROCK...
THE DEVIL'S BOTTLENECK... THE CAUSE OF OUR FAMOUS WIND! IT TRAPS THE AIR LIKE A NATURAL BELLOWS, AND PUSHES IT OUT AT GALE-FORCE STRENGTH!
I KNOW! BUT WHAT'S THAT MAST-THING YOU'VE BUILT ACROSS THE MOUTH OF IT?
AS WANGLER BLEW A SUDDEN BLAST ON HIS WHISTLE... THE MAYOR OF CHILBAY BEGAN TO FIND OUT...
ALL TOGETHER, LADS... HEEEAAVE!
PHEEEEEP!
BY JOVE! CONCEALED TEAMS, GOING INTO ACTION! BUT WHAT ARE THEY HOISTING UP THE MAST?

... IT'S A MASSIVE SAIL! IT FITS ACROSS THE MOUTH OF THE BOTTLENECK!
THAT'S RIGHT, SIR! IT'S A SORT OF GIANT DRAUGHT-EXCLUDER!
AS THE SHRIEKING GALE WAS SUDDENLY CUTOFF...
HEY PRESTO! ALL FALL DOWN! GET THE IDEA, MR. MAYOR!
GRUMPF!
FLOMMMPF!
THE WIND STOPPED WHEN YOU LEAST EXPECTED IT, SO YOU LOST YOUR BALANCE! THINK WHAT'LL HAPPEN TO THE SLOGGERS, WHEN WE PLAY THE SAME TRICKON THEM!
OF COURSE! HOW FIENDISHLY SIMPLE! YOU'RE A GENIUS, WANGLER! THE CUP IS AS GOOD AS OURS!
THE FOLLOWING DAY, UNAWARE OF REG WANGLER'S TREACHEROUS PLAN, THOUSANDS OF 'WHAT-A-LARK FANS TURNED UP FOR THE LONG-AWAITED FINAL...
WHEEEEEEE-EEE
STONE ME! THE CHILBAY WIND IS BLOWING HARDER THAN EVER TODAY!
SLOG IT TO 'EM, SLUDGEMOUTH!
BUT, LOOK ... THE SLOGGERS SEEM TO BE REVELLING IN IT! THEY'RE COMING OUT BACKWARDS!
EVEN BILLY BORING HAD TO SHOUT TO MAKE HIMSELF HEARD...
CHILBAY
SLUDGEMOUTH
JUST THOUGHT I'D 'BREEZE IN', FOLKS! HA, HA! HEEE! AND HERE WE GO FOR THE FIRST EVENT... A GIANT EGG-AND-SPOON RACE! TWO POINTS TO THE WINNERS! ARE YOU READY, WHAT-A-LARKERS...?
THEY'RE OFF! SLUDGEMOUTH! SLUDGEMOUTH!
BLAM!
CHILBAY
SLUDGEMOUTH
CLOBBER THEM, CHILBAY!

LEANING INTO THE COLOSSAL, HOWLING WIND, THE SLOGGERS WENT OFF WITH CAREFULLY-TIMED PRECISION...
THEY'RE IN THE LEAD ALREADY!
BUT NOT FOR LONG, HEH, HEH! NOW TO START COUNTING THE SECONDS! ONE, TWO, THREE...
AN INSTANT LATER, AS THE BLAST OF A WHISTLE REACHED THE WAITING SAIL-HOISTERS...
THERE'S THE SIGNAL! TO THE ROPES, MEN! HOIST THAT SAIL...
THE CHILBAY WIND SUDDENLY VANISHED LIKE MAGIC...
EVERYONE'S FALLING LIKE NINE-PINS! AND SO ARE THE SLOGGERS!
WUUAAH!
GRRRF!
BUT THE CHILBAY TEAM-MEMBERS, KNOWING WHAT TO EXPECT, HAD BRACED THEMSELVES ACCORDINGLY...
THEY MANAGED TO KEEP THEIR BALANCE... THEY'VE WON!
FIRST BLOOD TO CHILBAY! HURRAAAY!
AS SUDDENLY AS IT HAD STOPPED, THE DREADED WIND BLEW UP AGAIN...
HOW ABOUT THAT? MUST BE FREAK WEATHER CONDITIONS, FOLKS! HEEE, WHAT A LARK! BUT ON TO THE NEXT EVENT, WHICH IS THE WATER-MARATHON!
TWO GIANT PAIRS OF SCALES HAD BEEN ERECTED AT THE TOP OF A WOODEN RAMP...
EACH TEAM WILL RACE TO FILL THE LEFT-HAND SCALE-BUCKETS WITH WATER... UNTIL THE WEIGHT OF IT CAUSES THE OTHER BUCKET TO RISE INTO THE AIR, TAKING A MEMBER OF THE TEAM WITH IT...
THE FIRST TEAM TO GET THEIR BALL INTO THE NET, WINS TWO MORE POINTS!
TED LARKIN YELLED TO HIS TEAM-MATES, AS THE AMAZING MARATHON BEGAN...
THE WIND'S BEHIND US, THIS TIME... SO LEAN RIGHT BACK! WE DON'T WANT TO OVERSHOOT THE TOP OF THE RAMP!

BUT, ONCE AGAIN, WITHOUT WARNING...
THE WIND'S... S-STOPPED AGAIN! LOOK OUT!
GLUB!
WAAAH!
THE SLOGGERS HAVE GOT TO START AGAIN ... BUT CHILBAY ARE STILL GOING!
THEY WERE LEANING FORWARD WHEN THE WIND STOPPED!
THE SHATTERED SLOGGERS DIDN'T KNOW WHAT HAD HIT THEM...
AND LONG BEFORE THE SLOGGERS COULD MAKE UP FOR LOST GROUND...
UP GO THE SCALES... AND THERE GOES THE BALL INTO THE NET!
CHILBAY HAVE DONE IT AGAIN! HURRAAAY!
ZWOINNNG
FOUR POINTS DOWN, WITH ONLY TWO EVENTS TO COME! I...I RECKON WE'VE HAD IT, LADS!
CHILBAY 4
WHY SHOULD THE WIND KEEP STOPPING AND STARTING? IT'S NEVER BEEN SO ERRATIC BEFORE!
THAT'S WHAT I WAS THINKING, FLIPPER! AND THERE'S SOMETHING ELSE I'VE NOTICED...
... APART FROM THE MEMBERS OF HIS TEAM, REG WANGLER IS THE ONLY PERSON WHO IS MANAGING TO KEEP HIS BALANCE, AS IF HE KNOWS EXACTLY WHEN THE WIND IS GOING TO STOP! THIS NEEDS LOOKING INTO, SLOGGERS!
TAKING COVER BEHIND ONE OF THE STANDS, THE SLOGGERS SWUNG INTO ACTION...
HURRY, LADS! FACE INTO THE WIND! I'LL USE THE BINOCULARS!
HEAT
2·15
D-DON'T DROP US, CHARLIE ANVIL!
NO EXIT
THE CHILBAY WIND STARTED UP AGAIN, JUST AS TED REACHED THE TOP...
IT MUST BE SOMETHING TO DO WITH WHERE THE WIND IS COMING FROM! HOLD STEADY, LADS!
CAN YOU SEE ANYTHING, TED?

YOU BET I CAN! SO THAT'S IT! RIGHT, MR. WANGLER... WE'LL SOON PUT SOME WIND IN YOUR SAILS!
A FEW MOMENTS LATER, TO THE AMAZEMENT OF THE WHOLE CROWD...
... AND HERE'S A SENSATION, FOLKS! SLUDGEMOUTH HAVE PLAYED THEIR TRUMP-CARD!
CRIKEY! THIS MEANS THAT IF THE SLOGGERS LOSE THIS EVENT, THE CUP GOES TO CHILBAY, NO MATTER HOW MANY EVENTS ARE LEFT!
BUT IF SLUDGEMOUTH WIN... THEY GET DOUBLE BONUS POINTS!
REG WANGLER CHUCKLED TRIUMPHANTLY...
LARKIN'S LOONIES ARE GAMBLING IN VAIN, MR. MAYOR! I'VE TOLD OUR TEAM TO BE READY FOR ANOTHER WIND-STOP... SIXTY SECONDS FROM NOW!
BUT AS USUAL, SLUDGEMOUTH WON'T BE EXPECTING IT! THEY'LL FALL LIKE A TON OF BRICKS!
THE MAYOR WASN'T JOKING...
HERE THEY GO FOR THE THIRD EVENT... A GIANT FOUR-MAN STILT-RACE!
BANG
THE SLOGGERS HAVE LEFT OUT CHARLIE ANVIL, THEIR STRONGEST MAN! I WONDER WHERE HE IS...?
THWAAAAACK
AT THAT MOMENT, THE SLUDGEMOUTH BLACKSMITH WAS RIGHT BEHIND REG WANGLER...
UUU-UUULF!
YOUR TEAM BE DOIN' ROIGHT FOINE, TODAY, MR. WANGLER! ACCEPT MOI 'GRATULASHUNS!
OH, N-NO! YOU...FOOL! PREEEP! YOU HIT ME SO... PREEP... HARD ON THE BACK, I'VE SWALLOWED ME WHISTLE! PREEEP!
AS WANGLER'S UNINTENTIONAL SIGNAL TRAVELLED ALONG HIS LINE OF HELPERS, AND REACHED THE DEVIL'S BOTTLENECK...
PREEEEEEP!
RIGHT, MEN... HAUL AWAY FOR CHILBAY! SEAL UP THE BOTTLENECK!
HEEE-AAVE!

A FEW SECONDS LATER...
GOOD GRIEF, THE WIND'S STOPPED! REG GAVE THE SIGNAL TOO EARLY!
WE WEREN'T READY FOR IT!
H-HELP!
IT WAS A TOTAL COLLAPSE OF THE CHILBAY TEAM...
BUT THE SLOGGERS WERE READY...
YIPPEE! WE DONE IT, LADS! DOUBLE BONUS POINTS!
CHILBAY NEVER RECOVERED FROM THEIR SHOCK DEFEAT. AND AFTER THE SLOGGERS HAD ROMPED AWAY WITH THE NEXT AND LAST EVENT...
...THE CUP'S YOURS, TED! AND NOW I CALL UPON REG WANGLER, TO LEAD THE CHILBAY TEAM IN A SPORTING CHEER, FOR THE NEW WESTERN REGION WHAT-A-LARK CHAMPIONS!
I DON'T THINK REG COULD EVEN MANAGE A BOO AT THE MOMENT, BILLY!
PREEEP! UUURGLE... GLUB!
...HE SEEMS TO BE SUFFERING FROM AN ATTACK OF THE WIND!
HA, HA, HA!
THE END.

? DO YOU KNOW ?

1. Why can't this be the Statue of Justice on London's Old Bailey ?

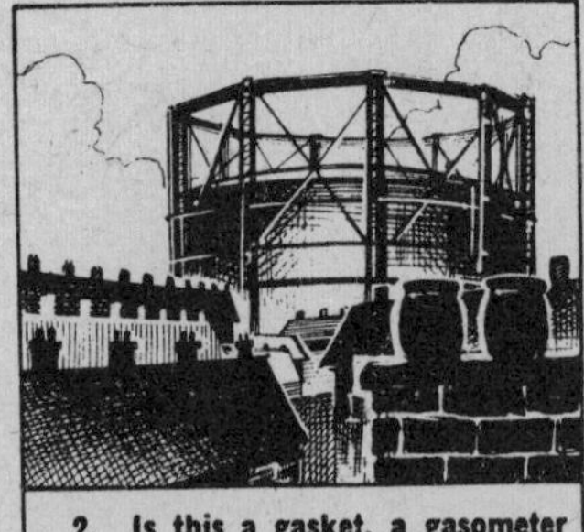

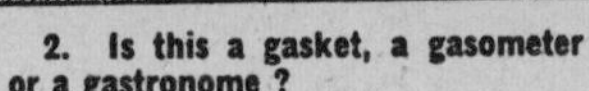

2. Is this a gasket, a gasometer or a gastronome ?

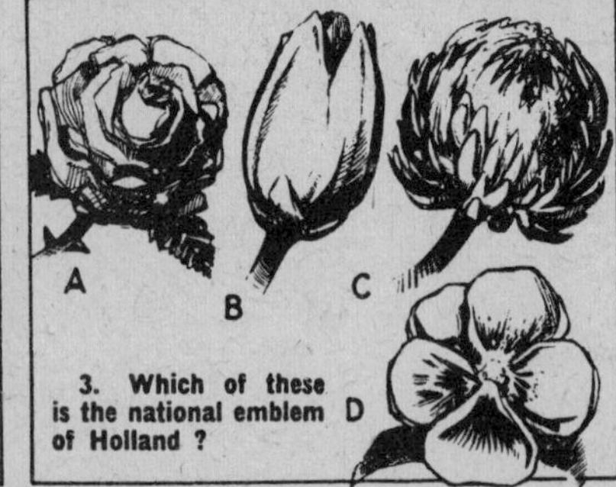

3. Which of these is the national emblem of Holland ?

4. Which of these weapons is a boomerang ?

5. One is the Victoria Cross—but which ? And what are the others ?

ANSWERS TO THE QUIZ
(Turn the page upside down to read the solution.)

1. Because it is blind-folded.
2. It is sometimes called a gasometer, but its correct name is 'gasholder.'
3. B. The tulip.
4. They are all boomerangs.
5. 'A' is the Victoria Cross ; 'B' the M.C. (Military Cross) ; 'C' is the D.F.C. (Distinguished Flying Cross).

JEST A MINUTE!

BALA the BRITON

LONG, LONG AGO, THE WARRIOR GODS SENT BALA, SON OF HARAL, ON A QUEST TO FIND HIS FATHER. WITH HIS CREW OF BRITONS, AND A STRANGE AND WISE OLD MAN CALLED THE ROON, HE SAILED INTO MANY UNCHARTED SEAS... AND TO PERILS NEVER BEFORE ENCOUNTERED BY MORTAL MAN. FROM THE LOOKOUT HIGH ON THE MAST OF THE BRITONS' DRAGON SHIP CAME A JOYOUS CRY...
BALA! LAND!
AT LAST! WE'VE BEEN AT SEA FOR TWENTY DAYS AND MORE! IT WILL FEEL GOOD TO HAVE THE EARTH BENEATH US AGAIN!
WE CAN TAKE IN FRESH WATER, LUSCIOUS FRUITS FROM THE TREES...

BUT THE ROON SHOOK HIS WISE AND ANCIENT HEAD...
THAT IS THE SHINING ISLAND, THE HOME OF THE FAVOURED ONES. THE GODS HAVE SWORN TO DESTROY ANY WHO TRY TO LAND THERE BALA!
THE FAVOURED ONES? AND WHO ARE THEY, ROON?

THEY ARE A RACE OF NOBLE PEOPLE CALLED THE CHIVALS. SO GALLANT AND GOOD ARE THEY... THAT THE WARRIOR GODS GAVE THEM THIS SHINING ISLAND... AND THE BLESSING OF ALMOST ETERNAL YOUTH!

THE FAVOURED ONES! THEY... AND THAT ISLE GIVEN THEM BY THE GODS... MUST BE A WONDROUS SIGHT TO BEHOLD!
YES, BALA! BUT A SIGHT THAT NEITHER YOU NOR ANY OTHER MORTAL MAN WILL SEE!

SUDDENLY, THE AIR FILLED WITH A SOUND LIKE A THOUSAND SWEET LYRES...
WHOOOOOOOOOOOOO!
IT COMES FROM THE ISLAND... IT MUST BE THE MUSIC OF THE GODS!
IT IS... LULLING... US TO... SLEEP!

SOON, ONLY ONE MAN WAS AWAKE...
BALAA-BALAAAAA!
THE MUSIC... IS CALLING ME! BY THE GODS... A BIRD IS COMING FROM THE ISLAND!

ITS GREAT WINGS BEATING THE CRYSTAL AIR, THE GIANT BIRD TOOK BALA BY THE SHOULDERS–AND...
CRAAARR!
IT...IT'S CARRYING ME AWAY... YET I HAVE NO FEAR OF IT!

ONLY WHEN THE BIRD BEGAN TO GLIDE DOWN TO THE SHINING ISLAND DID BALA FEEL AFRAID...
THE FAVOURED ONES! ROON SAID THE GODS DECREED THAT NO MAN SHALL GAZE UPON THEM!

BUT MOMENTS LATER...
I... I MUSTN'T LET MYSELF SEE THEM!
DO NOT SHIELD YOUR EYES, BALA, SON OF HAR'AL! LOOK AT US!

BALA COULD NOT RESTRAIN A GASP...
IT... IT CAN'T BE THEM! ROON SAID THE GODS GAVE THEM ETERNAL YOUTH! THESE ARE OLD, OLD MEN!
BEHOLD US, BALA! WE ARE THE FAVOURED ONES! THE GODS HAVE SENT YOU TO HELP US!

THE GODS GAVE US THE MAGICAL RAINBOW CLOAK... THE MANY-COLOURED MANTLE OF YOUTH! WHILE I WORE IT WE REMAINED YOUNG... BUT IT HAS BEEN STOLEN FROM US!
AND NOW AGE COMES SWIFTLY! EACH DAY IS LIKE A YEAR OF TIME! SOON... UNLESS YOU CAN SAVE US... WE SHALL DIE!

AN EVIL SORCERER HAS TAKEN THE RAINBOW CLOAK TO THE TOP OF THAT MOUNTAIN! WE ARE TOO WEAK AND FEEBLE TO GET IT BACK!
SAY NO MORE! I WILL BRING IT BACK TO YOU!

THERE ARE TERRIBLE DANGERS, BALA! THE GRAWK-BIRD HAS NEITHER RENDING CLAWS NOR HOOKED BEAK TO HELP YOU FIGHT THEM! BUT THE GRAWK CAN WARN YOU OF DANGER!

HALFWAY UP THE MOUNTAIN, BALA MET THE FIRST PERIL...
CRAAAK
GROORGH!

A LONG HIDEOUS TONGUE FLICKED OUT WITH THE BLURRING SPEED OF A STRIKING COBRA ...
UUOOOORGH!
I'VE LOST MY SWORD!

CRAAWK
GROOO!

THEN, EVEN AS DEATH LOOMED ABOVE HIM...
CRAAAWK!
WHUNK!
GROOGH
THE GRAWK HAS SAVED ME! NOW I HAVE A CHANCE!

AND AS THE BEAST SNAPPED AT THE FLUTTERING GRAWK...
GROOAAGH!
DIE, DEMON BEAST!

CRAAAR!
O BRAVE AND LOYAL GRAWK-BIRD! I SEE WHY THE FAVOURED ONES MUST LOVE YOU!

BUT, FURTHER ON, WHERE THE PATH BECAME A BRIDGE ACROSS A DEEP RAVINE...
RIIIRR!
THIS MONSTER IS TRULY TERRIBLE TO BEHOLD! NO SWORD WILL PENETRATE THAT SHELL! YET I MUST CROSS THIS BRIDGE!
CLICK! CLICK!

CLICK!
RIIIRR!
CLICK!
THERE IS BUT ONE WAY!

CRAAAR!
GRAWK! SAVE ME!
RIIIRR!

THE GRAWK DID NOT FAIL BALA...
CRAAARR!
THERE IS THE TOP, GRAWK-BIRD! LET US PRAY THAT THE SORCERER DOES NOT YET KNOW OF OUR COMING!

ON THE MIST-SHROUDED SUMMIT, THE GALLANT BRITON SAW...
THAT MUST BE THE SORCERER ASLEEP! BUT WHERE IS THE RAINBOW CLOAK? I CANNOT SEE IT!

BUT EVEN AS BALA BEGAN TO SEARCH...
YOU CAME FOR THE RAINBOW CLOAK? YOU ARE A BRAVE MAN... BUT A FOOL! ALL YOU WILL FIND IS DEATH!

I AM NOT ALONE, BRAVE-BUT-FOOLISH-ONE! I WILL LEAVE IT TO THE ROTH TO KILL YOU!
ROOORGH!

BUT THOUGH BALA KNEW HIS DOOM WAS SEALED...
THEN I SHALL DIE FIGHTING... AS A BRITON SHOULD!
SNICK!
FOOL! YOU CANNOT SLAY ME WITH A ... OH, NO! NO!

ROOOGH!
CRAAHR!
NO, NO! DON'T TAKE IT AWAAAAAAAAAY!
THE RAG HAS FALLEN OVER THE GRAWK'S HEAD!

NEXT MOMENT, BALA FELT THAT HE MUST BE DREAMING...
NO, NO! NOOOOOO!
THE SORCERER IS FADING AWAY! AND THE BEAST... THE ROTH... IS TURNING INTO A SKELETON!

THEN, FROM ABOVE, CAME A BLAZE OF COLOUR...
RAARK!
THE RAG THE SORCERER WAS WEARING... HAS CHANGED INTO THE RAINBOW CLOAK! THE RAG WAS REALLY THE MANTLE OF YOUTH!

AN SO...
THE SORCERER HAD HIDDEN IT WELL... BY GIVING IT THE APPEARANCE OF A RAG CLOAK!
THE ...THE MANTLE! I MUST PUT IT ON!

HARDLY HAD THE SHIMMERING CLOAK BEEN FASTENED ROUND THE SHOULDERS OF THE LEADER OF THE FAVOURED ONES, WHEN...
NOW, BALA, YOU SEE US AS THE GODS WISHED TO KEEP US! AND YOUR FRIEND... THE GRAWK... LOOK AT HIM NOW!

THEN, ONCE AGAIN, BALA FOUND HIMSELF BORNE THROUGH THE AIR...
FAREWELL, BALA! SOON YOUR SAILORS WILL AWAKE FROM THEIR SLEEP!

AS THE DRAGON-SHIP SAILED ON, ONLY THE WISE ROON KNEW WHAT HAD HAPPENED...
I THINK, BALA, SON OF HARAL, THAT YOU HAVE BEEN GRANTED A WONDER DENIED TO ALL OTHER MEN!
NO MATTER WHAT HARDSHIPS I SHALL HAVE TO FACE IN THE FUTURE ... I HAVE HAD MY REWARD, ROON!

I SAW THEM... THE FAVOURED ONES!
The End

? DO YOU KNOW ?

1. Name the sea in which it is possible to sit down and read a book without sinking !
2. One is a lama, and the other is a llama. Which is which ?
3. Where does this car come from ?
GBJ
4. What can you tell when you see a ship flying a blue and white flag like this ?
5. What is this punch called ? And is it a foul ?
6. It could never happen in Africa. Why not ?
7. Is this man pulling a rickshaw, a sampan, or a pagoda ?
8. See anything wrong ?
9. Are these soldiers Askaris, Mahouts or Gurkhas ? And are they holding cutlasses, kukris, or scimitars ?
ANSWERS TO THE QUIZ
(Turn the page upside down to read them)
1. The Dead Sea. There is so much salt in the water, a man cannot sink in it. 2. The animal is the llama, the man is a lama. 3. Jersey, Channel Islands. 4. That the ship is about to sail. It is the Blue Peter. 5. Rabbit punch—and it *is* a foul. 6. Because there are no tigers in Africa ! 7. A rickshaw. 8. Penguins do not fly. 9. A Gurkha holding a kukri.

THE PHANTOM VIKING

...AND BOTH TEAMS CHARGED OVER HIM!
TRUST OLD LOOPY TO GET IN THE WAY! HA! HA!
GUUUGH!

SO IT WAS THAT OLAF LARSEN HAD TO GO TO BED FOR A FEW DAYS WITH A SPRAINED BACK, TWISTED ANKLE AND VARIOUS ASSORTED BRUISES. GOOD-NATURED HELEN YATES, THE HEADMASTER'S SECRETARY, CAME TO VISIT HIM...
YOU'VE GOT THE TELEVISION AND I'VE BROUGHT YOU A FEW BOOKS TO KEEP YOU AMUSED. HONESTLY, OLAF, YOU SHOULD BE MORE CAREFUL. YOU KNOW YOU'RE NOT STRONG ENOUGH TO GET MIXED UP WITH THOSE YOUNG RUFFIANS!

THAT NIGHT A GALE RAGED IN THE NORTH SEA, AND THE SIX CROOKS WATCHED FROM THE DECK OF A POWERFUL MOTOR LAUNCH.
HERE SHE COMES!
...THE NETHERLAND FLYER!
WE'VE MOVED THE BUOYS MARKING THE SANDBANK—SHE'LL STRIKE ANY MOMENT NOW!

THEN IT HAPPENED— WITH A SHOCK THAT SHOOK EVERY RIVET, THE BIG SHIP SMASHED INTO THE SANDBANK AND DROVE HERSELF AGROUND...
WE'RE AGROUND!

THE RADIO OPERATOR BEGAN TO TAP OUT A FRANTIC S.O.S. —UNTIL A HAIL OF MACHINE GUN BULLETS TORE INTO THE SIDE OF HIS CABIN...
UUUGH!

TEN MINUTES LATER THE NEWS REACHED OLAF LARSEN LYING IN HIS BED...
WE INTERRUPT THIS PROGRAMME WITH A NEWS FLASH. A SHIP IS IN PERIL IN THE ENGLISH CHANNEL. AN S.O.S. MESSAGE HAS BEEN RECEIVED, BUT WAS CUT OFF BEFORE THE OPERATOR COULD GIVE HIS POSITION...

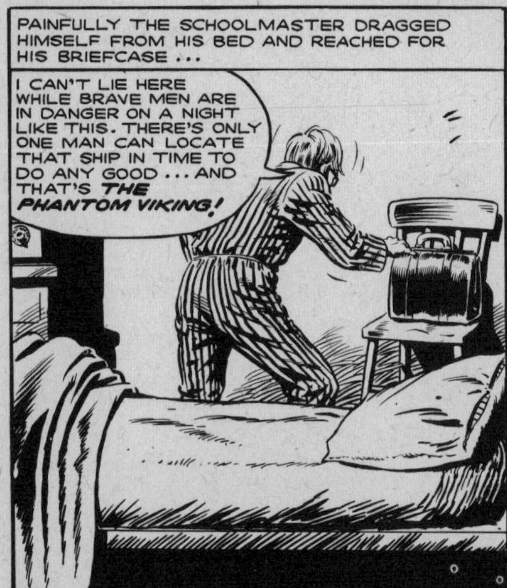
PAINFULLY THE SCHOOLMASTER DRAGGED HIMSELF FROM HIS BED AND REACHED FOR HIS BRIEFCASE...
I CAN'T LIE HERE WHILE BRAVE MEN ARE IN DANGER ON A NIGHT LIKE THIS. THERE'S ONLY ONE MAN CAN LOCATE THAT SHIP IN TIME TO DO ANY GOOD...AND THAT'S THE PHANTOM VIKING!

FROM THE CASE HE CAREFULLY WITHDREW A VIKING HELMET— AND AS HE PUT IT ON AN INCREDIBLE CHANGE CAME OVER HIM...
I FEEL THE FANTASTIC POWER OF MY MIGHTY ANCESTORS!

NEXT SECOND, THE PHANTOM VIKING WAS STREAKING THROUGH THE GALE-TORN NIGHT...
FIRST... TO FIND THAT SHIP!

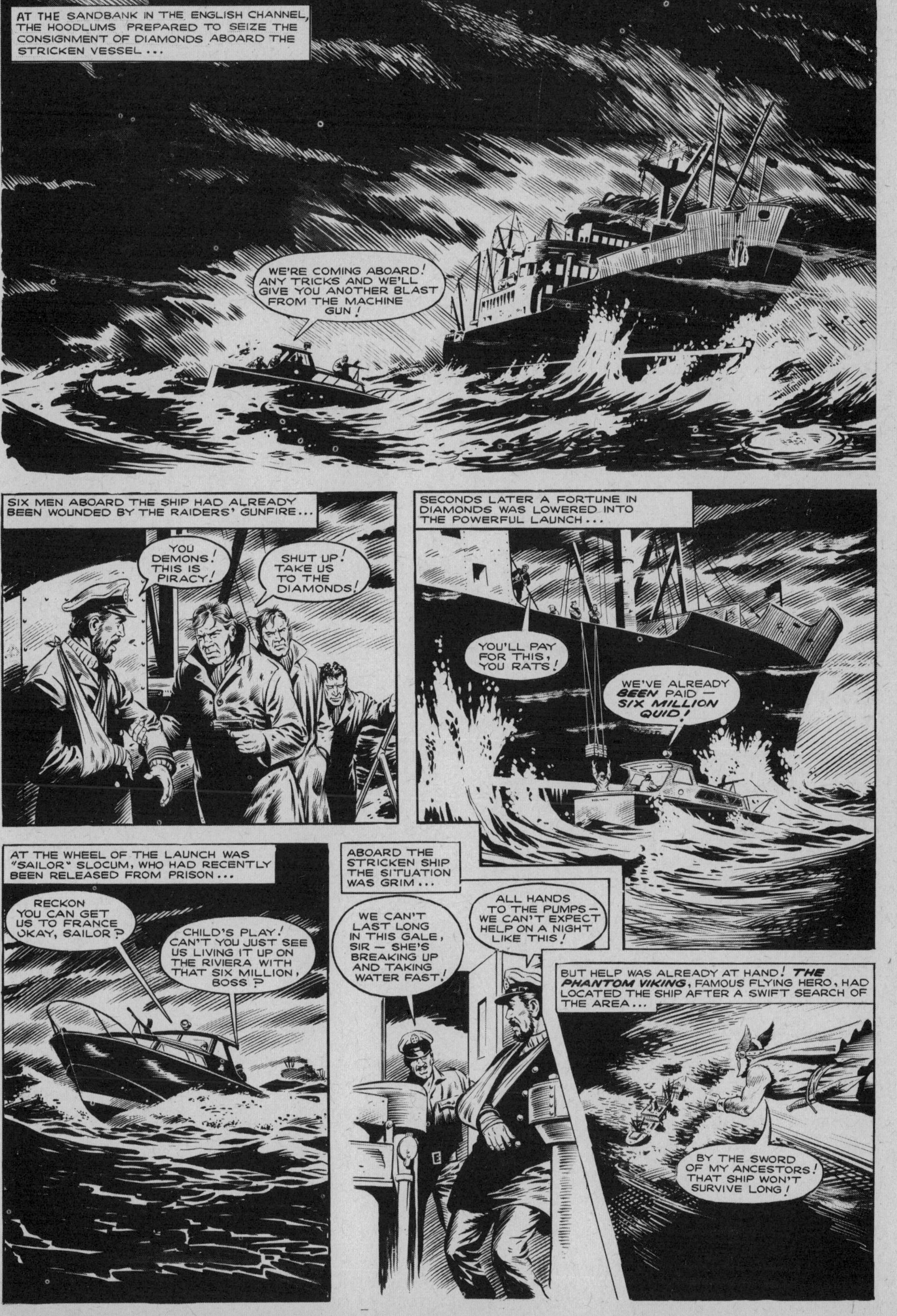

SIX MEN ABOARD THE SHIP HAD ALREADY BEEN WOUNDED BY THE RAIDERS' GUNFIRE...

YOU DEMONS! THIS IS PIRACY!

SHUT UP! TAKE US TO THE DIAMONDS!

SECONDS LATER A FORTUNE IN DIAMONDS WAS LOWERED INTO THE POWERFUL LAUNCH...

YOU'LL PAY FOR THIS, YOU RATS!

WE'VE ALREADY *BEEN* PAID — ***SIX MILLION QUID!***

AT THE WHEEL OF THE LAUNCH WAS "SAILOR" SLOCUM, WHO HAD RECENTLY BEEN RELEASED FROM PRISON...

RECKON YOU CAN GET US TO FRANCE OKAY, SAILOR?

CHILD'S PLAY! CAN'T YOU JUST SEE US LIVING IT UP ON THE RIVIERA WITH THAT SIX MILLION, BOSS?

ABOARD THE STRICKEN SHIP THE SITUATION WAS GRIM...

WE CAN'T LAST LONG IN THIS GALE, SIR — SHE'S BREAKING UP AND TAKING WATER FAST!

ALL HANDS TO THE PUMPS — WE CAN'T EXPECT HELP ON A NIGHT LIKE THIS!

BUT HELP WAS ALREADY AT HAND! ***THE PHANTOM VIKING***, FAMOUS FLYING HERO, HAD LOCATED THE SHIP AFTER A SWIFT SEARCH OF THE AREA...

BY THE SWORD OF MY ANCESTORS! THAT SHIP WON'T SURVIVE LONG!

THE SHIP'S CAPTAIN TURNED, A FEW MOMENTS LATER, AND GASPED TO SEE THE TALL, STRANGE FIGURE ON HIS BRIDGE...
AAH — WHO THE BLAZES...?
THESE BULLET HOLES... WHAT HAS HAPPENED ON BOARD THIS SHIP, CAPTAIN?

TERSELY, THE CAPTAIN EXPLAINED...
...THEN THE RATS LEFT WITH THE DIAMONDS. THEY WERE HEADING FOR THE FRENCH COAST... AND NOW THIS SHIP'S SINKING AND I'VE GOT SIX BADLY INJURED MEN WHO CAN'T BE MOVED!
THEN THERE'S ONLY ONE THING TO DO!

SOARING INTO THE AIR OVER THE SHIP'S BOWS, THE PHANTOM VIKING GRABBED A HEAVY HAWSER...
BY THUNDER— WHAT IS HE? A MAN OR...

EXERTING ALL HIS FANTASTIC POWER, THE VIKING DRAGGED THE VESSEL FROM THE MERCILESS GRIP OF THE SANDBANK...
HERE SHE COMES NOW!

THE CREW WATCHED IN AWE AS THEY FELT THEIR SHIP MOVE SLOWLY FORWARD INTO THE TEETH OF THE GALE...
HE—HE'S TAKING US TO ENGLAND!
DON'T STAND THERE GAWPING— MAN THE PUMPS BEFORE THE WHOLE SHIP GOES DOWN UNDER US!

EARLY THE FOLLOWING MORNING THE PHANTOM VIKING PULLED THE VESSEL TO THE ENGLISH SHORE...
HEY— DON'T GO!
FAREWELL— MY TASK ISN'T FINISHED YET

TURNING, THE VIKING STREAKED ACROSS THE CHANNEL — BUT SUDDENLY...
I HOPE I FIND THOSE CROOKS QUICKLY — BECAUSE THE WIND IS BEGINNING TO CHANGE!

INSIDE THE VIKING HELMET WAS THIS WARNING: WHEN THE WIND FROM THE SOUTH DOTH BLOW, THE ANCIENT VIKING POWER SHALL GO! AND A FEW MOMENTS LATER — THE WIND BLEW FROM THE SOUTH!
AAAGH!
THE PHANTOM VIKING WAS CHANGED BACK INTO OLAF LARSEN, A WEAK, HELPLESS SCHOOLMASTER, FALLING OUT OF THE SKY!

OLAF LARSEN WAS SPOTTED BY A PASSING TRAWLER ...
MAN IN THE WATER!
HEEEEELP!

MEANWHILE THE LAUNCH CONTAINING THE SIX DIAMOND THIEVES HAD REACHED A DESOLATE PART OF THE FRENCH COAST ...
THERE'S OUR PLANE!

BESIDE THE PLANE A HARD-EYED MAN WAS WAITING ...
AS ARRANGED, M'SIEU, THIS WILL COST YOU FIVE THOUSAND POUNDS!
TAKE IT IN DIAMONDS, AND LET'S GO!

THE AIRCRAFT TOOK OFF, HEADING SOUTH ... BUT THE WHOLE EPISODE HAD BEEN OBSERVED BY AN OLD FRENCH FARMER ...
MA FOI — THOSE MEN — ASSUREDLY THEY ARE CRIMINALS — SMUGGLERS, PERHAPS!

MEANWHILE, OLAF WAS SHIVERING MISERABLY BELOW DECKS IN THE TRAWLER ...
I SUPPOSE YOU WERE TRYING TO SWIM THE CHANNEL. BEATS ME WHY A WEEDY CHAP LIKE YOU SHOULD TRY IT!

WELL, I'D BEST BE GETTING BACK ON DECK. THE WIND'S CHANGING AGAIN AND I RECKON THE GALE'S GOING TO GET WORSE BEFORE IT GETS BETTER.
THE WIND — CHANGING!

LEFT ALONE, OLAF LARSEN SWIFTLY PUT ON HIS PRECIOUS HELMET — AND AT ONCE BECAME THE PHANTOM VIKING!
NOW THE WIND IS NO LONGER IN THE SOUTH MY POWER HAS RETURNED! I CAN CONTINUE THE PURSUIT!

MINUTES LATER, THE DEMORALISED CROOKS PILED OUT OF THE LANDED AIRCRAFT AND SHRANK IN TERROR BEFORE THE STERN GAZE OF THE PHANTOM VIKING...

RIGHT, I'M TAKING YOU ALL TO THE POLICE!

WHEN THE THIEVES WERE SAFELY IN CUSTODY, THE AMAZING VIKING RETURNED TO ENGLAND AND AGAIN BECAME OLAF LARSEN, WHO HAD BEEN RECOVERING FROM ILLNESS IN THE SCHOOL SICK BAY. LATER...

HERE IS THE NEWS: *THE THIEVES WHO STOLE DIAMONDS VALUED AT SIX MILLION POUNDS HAVE BEEN ARRESTED. DETAILS OF THEIR CAPTURE HAVE NOT BEEN REVEALED, BUT ARE BELIEVED TO HAVE VARIOUS UNUSUAL FACTORS...*

...AND OLAF LARSEN, THE WEAK SCHOOLMASTER, SMILED!

"RECKON we fell for it like a load of suckers, Lootenant. And now we're in a spot we'll be darn lucky to get out of!"

"We sure did, Colonel! Nobody told us this island of Tipi-Tapu was swarming with Nips!"

Sweating, dust-streaked, Colonel Wilbur Dogie, of the U.S. Marine Corps, had been in many tight spots during the ferocious Pacific War against the Japanese in 1944.

He and his men had spearheaded many attacks, storming ashore against vicious and deadly opposition. The landing on Tipi-Tapu had been different. The Pacific Fleet was forging ahead, by-passing smaller islands, heading for the main Japanese bases, leaving the smaller pockets of Japanese to be mopped-up later.

Colonel Dogie's outfit had been detailed to occupy and hold this spot in the ocean, one of the countless islands of the Pacific.

Not until the landing ships had moved on had the Japanese started shooting. Colonel Dogie and his men had fought a running battle in the jungle, and now they were penned in a clearing, luckily with a running stream to give them water, surrounded by dense thickets of tall bamboo, each one fifty feet high and as thick as a man's leg.

They could not see the Japs, and the enemy could not see them. But they knew they were surrounded. Once again came a swishing through the air, and an ear-splitting crack. A mortar bomb had soared over the bamboos and burst on the edge of the clearing where Colonel Dogie's men, some wounded, all exhausted, sprawled in their foxholes.

It was a matter of time.

Colonel Dogie knew he had only one chance.

"Any further word about that British outfit that's supposed to be on its way to help us, Hank?" he asked the lean-faced young lieutenant who crouched by a radio set.

"No, Colonel," said Lieutenant Hank Garner. "A Limey unit is on its way from New Guinea, that's all we know. They've done great work with the Australians, so the word goes. So we've just gotta wait!"

"I suppose those Nips'll keep themselves hidden again," Colonel Dogie growled. "They'll let the Limeys land, then open up."

He squinted up at the sky, all they could see from the densely-surrounded clearing. "Darn lucky for us the Japs don't seem to be able to spare any Zeros or bombers. The Fleet's keepin' those busy!"

Suddenly faces turned up as they heard an increasing drone.

"It's them, sir!" Hank Garner barked excitedly. "I'm getting their signals!"

A Dakota passed over the clearing, and the Americans saw four falling objects turn into blossoming parachutes. The plane droned on as the four parachutists swayed down.

"This is nuts!" gasped Colonel Dogie. "Only one plane! Only four men! Those Limeys have let me down! What doggone use will *four men* be to us?"

"They'll be lucky to hit this clearing," said Hank. "Heck, it must look like a postage stamp from up there!"

But the besieged Americans need not have worried. The four parachutists were exceptional men. Their fighting qualities and talents were so strong and varied that they had been formed into a four-man special unit of the British Army!

They were the famous Sergeants Four—'Taffy' Jones, Alf Higgs, Jock McGill and Paddy O'Boyle—who had carried out many successful and seemingly impossible missions against Nazi and Jap alike.

Skilfully the four manoeuvered their parachutes, heading down towards the clearing.

"Stone me, I don't see any perishin' Japs!" said Cockney Alf Higgs.

"They'll be well hidden in the jungle, bach," said Welshman Taffy Jones. "I can see the Yanks, look you!"

"Och, it's a nasty position they're in," boomed Jock McGill, who had been a Highland gillie and stalker before he joined the Army. "Vairy difficult for them to make a move!"

"Bedad, we'll soon have those boyos out," said the giant Irishman, Paddy O'Boyle. "That is, if the Nips

The American troops watched in astonishment as the relief force floated down into the clearing. There were only four men!

don't start shootin' at us. Have yez thought that we're sitting targets up here?"

The lack of gunfire puzzled everyone. But down below, Japanese in hidden positions who had raised machine guns ready to shoot the four parachutists out of the sky, received sharp orders from Major Obashi, their commander.

"Don't shoot, fools!" the tough, scar-faced veteran barked. "It will give our positions away." He squinted through binoculars. "Ha, they are not Yankis. They are Tommees! Four more men to fall into our net!"

The Dakota had circled and was flying away. By the time it had gone, Sergeants Four had landed neatly and cleanly in the Americans' clearing, to the amazement of the battle-hardened veterans.

"For Pete's sake!" roared Colonel Dogie. "Where's the rest of the men? Command promised me *a whole British unit!*"

Alf Higgs saluted, grinning. "Colonel, you got your unit. It's us . . . at your service! No trouble too much for Sergeants Four!"

Jock McGill spoke to the goggling Marine Colonel.

"What escape plan had ye in mind, Colonel? Our briefing said ye were to be evacuated."

Colonel Dogie swallowed his anger. "Huh, the idea is we fight our way to a cove North of here . . . then radio, and a sub or PT boats will dash in to pick us up. All depends on whether we get there. No arrival, no boat. We're expendable, but the ships ain't. That's how it sizes up."

Heads ducked as a mortar bomb exploded high in the bamboos. Wicked splinters of bamboo showered down, but the four amazing British Sergeants did not turn a hair.

"Aiming at our voices," said Jock McGill. "Och, the Nips don't really know exactly where ye are, Colonel. So that helps."

"Yus, we better keep nice an' quiet," said Alf Higgs, thoughtfully studying the tall, dense growth of bamboos.

An amplified voice boomed out from somewhere in the jungle.

"Welcome to Tipi-Tapu, Tommees! You are foolish. You wish to commit hara-kiri—suicide? Four more heads will roll when we come to get the Yankis. Come and give yourselves up, and you will be treated as honourable plisoners!"

Paddy O'Boyle rumbled with laughter. "Bejabers, the little fella has a cheek on him! Me fist'll have the teeth out of his head when I meet him, so it will!"

Colonel Dogie watched amazed, rubbing his tired eyes, as Alf Higgs spoke quietly to Jock McGill.

"Get any direction from that voice, Jock?"

"Och, no, Alf. The loudspeaker'll be moving around, anyway, I'm thinking. We'll have to go out and find the main party."

"Nuts!" hissed Colonel Dogie. "Not even a snake can get through those doggone bamboos without making 'em rattle!"

"Dinna worry, sir," said Jock calmly. "We'll find a way! Ye've got an idea, Alf. I can see it glittering in your eyes."

"Let's have it, bach," said Taffy Jones.

"I was thinkin'," said Alf thoughtfully, "them there bamboos could come in mighty useful. Pin yer ears back an' listen to what's in me fertile brain!"

Stalking

Following Alf Higgs' instructions, the four Sergeants started cutting twenty-foot lengths of the thick bamboos.

"We'll make 'em into explosive javelins," he remarked calmly. "Taffy, you pack 'em with explosives, grenades, anything we got!"

"So what?" groaned Colonel Dogie. "We get a lot of bamboos full of explosives? You aim to blow a way through the bamboo jungle so we can get shot down by the Japs when we get out the other side?"

"No, sirree," Alf said perkily. "Old Paddy O'Boyle here is gonna throw the javelins *over the jungle* at the Japs. Reckon he can chuck 'em three hundred yards or more!"

"Sure! Tell me where the target is, and I'll be after hittin' it," said mighty Paddy O'Boyle, flexing his bulging arm muscles.

Jock McGill was tuning a walkie-talkie radio, ready to strap it on his back.

"I'll just go through and have a peek," the Scot said calmly. "I'll give ye the location of the main party, Paddy. Then, laddie, it's up to you!"

The baffled Americans stared as Jock made for the bamboos, dropped down, and slithered away like a

Paddy O'Boyle threw the heavy length of bamboo into the air with the skill of an expert javelin thrower.

The explosive-laden bamboo spears ringed the Jap force in a circle of shattering detonations that hurled them off their feet.

snake. In seconds he had gone, and there was not a sound to mark his stealthy progress through the dense growth. The bamboos grew so closely that the upper parts of those the Four had cut still hung suspended like a canopy overhead.

Taffy Jones was busy packing his bamboo bombs. Alf Higgs tuned another walkie-talkie set.

"He's a brave man," said Colonel Dogie wearily. "But those Japs are masters at jungle warfare. Your Scottish friend has gone to his death."

"Give over, Colonel," grinned Alf Higgs. "Jock was the greatest stalker in all Scotland! Those Japs won't hear 'im, see 'im, or even smell 'im! Honest, mate! All we got to do is wait until 'e pinpoints the position of the main party . . . then Paddy does 'is stuff!"

Somehow the weary Americans began to have faith in the amazing four sergeants. *These Limeys seemed to know their stuff.*

Jock McGill slithered onwards, and had covered more than two hundred yards when he caught the hissing sound of Japanese voices.

"Och, they give themselves away like a lot of snakes," he thought with a chuckle. "A body can hear 'em a mile away."

Jock was not doing justice to his own super-keen hearing. But the Japanese had no idea of his presence when he came to a more open part of the jungle, with scattered trees and rocks and undergrowth through which he wormed, watching the force which Major Obashi had gathered together.

The Jap officer was waving his sabre and shouting as soldiers lit flaming brands.

"We'll burn a way through the bamboos!" he ordered. "My patience is exhausted. We will fight our way through and kill the Yankis and their Tommee friends. Banzai!"

"Oho, so that's your idea!" thought Jock, and went to cover behind a rock, his stalker's mind estimating distances.

Then he spoke softly on his radio.

"Jock to Alf. Range three hundred yards, bearing two-five-oh! I'm thinking Paddy should be starting to let fly. The little men are starting a fire!"

Bamboo strike

Back in the clearing, Alf Higgs signalled to Paddy O'Boyle, who stood poised, holding one of the heavy lengths of bamboo. A quick glance at his compass, and Alf pointed out the direction.

Paddy O'Boyle drew back the huge, heavy bamboo, took a few steps forward, and launched it like a javelin thrower. The stunned Americans saw it soar away, high over the jungle.

"Jeepers, what a throw! That Mick's the strongest guy I've ever seen!"

Again and again Paddy hurled the bamboo javelins with their deadly loads. In his hiding place, Jock McGill chuckled as he saw them rain down, landing to stick in the soft earth, like a palisade around the startled Japanese soldiers. Men halted as they ran to fire the bamboos, with their brands.

But Major Obashi was laughing. "Victory is ours! The Yankis have run out of ammunition. Now they throw bamboos! They must be nearer than we thought. Get ready to charge, brave soldiers of Nippon!"

Then . . .BOOM! CRACK!

The time-fused explosives roared. Caught in a circle of shattering explosions, the Japs were hurled screaming off their feet. Trees flamed and undergrowth flared.

Major Obashi had been hurled yards away by the blast, still gripping his sabre, and knocked unconscious like many of his men.

Jock peered through the smoke, and spoke quietly into his radio transmitter.

"Dead on target, Paddy! I'm keeping the Japs covered, but there's no' many left, I'm thinking. Ye can come out now, fellers!"

Alf Higgs turned to the astonished Colonel Dogie.

"We're all set, Colonel. 'Ave to 'ack our way through, though."

"We go out, through that bamboo jungle? Heck, we'd be lost in minutes, feller!"

Taffy Jones chuckled. "Now, look you, Colonel bach, we're not so daft. Jock'll have left a marked trail as he went through. All we have to do is cut our way along it."

Cheering Americans rose. "Let's go, Colonel!"

"Heck, I'll sure be glad to get out of this hole in the little ole jungle!"

Paddy O'Boyle led the way, hacking left and right with a sharp machete. There was no need for the Americans to do anything but carry their equipment and weapons, as the massive Irishman hacked away. the bamboos falling to both sides of the tunnel he forged through them.

Jock McGill was found with his tommy-gun covering the few dazed Japanese survivors, who were busily quenching fires under his command.

"These characters have had enough, ma friends," he grinned. "But they say there's still a few more Nips roamin' in the gloamin'. Och, we'd better winkle 'em out before we can sit down in peace!"

The Sergeants Four led the jubilant Americans on a gun-toting tour of the small island. They fought many minor battles, until they were sure it was clear of Japs.

Then, down by a sandy beach, they found some huts and stores. Cleared of the enemy, Tipi-Tapu became an island paradise.

Jovially Alf Higgs took over the stores, dispensing food and drink to the exhausted Americans.

"Fellers, I got to say it," said Colonel Dogie, his voice breaking. "In all my combat experience, I've never met such guys as you! Doggone, we'd have been dead ducks in that lousy trap if you four geniuses hadn't come a-dropping out of the sky!"

"All in a day's work, Colonel," Alf chuckled. "I reckon we can make a nice little number for ourselves on this 'ere island."

"Indeed to goodness, there's no need to evacuate it now," said Taffy Jones. "Wouldn't it be a good idea now, Colonel, if you told your top-brass on the radio that it's cleared of the little yeller fellers . . . and you can hold it as a base?"

Colonel Dogie stared. "Say, that's a humdinger of an idea, Taffy, boyo!"

Some of the Americans were bathing off the gleaming sandy beach. Alf Higgs waved towards them.

"Ain't it peaceful, Colonel? I'd be glad to run it as a rest an' recreation centre for any of the Joes who can get a bit o' leave!"

Paddy O'Boyle was lying under a nearby tree, cracking open a coconut with his bare hands, as if it were a walnut.

"Bedad, oi've seen oislands like this in the fillums," he said contentedly. "Oi could end me days in peace here, so I could!"

"We'll stay here until the next job turns up," said Alf Higgs. "No need for any 'urry, is there, me old mates?"

"I've never met guys like you before," said Colonel Dogie. Alf Higgs chuckled.

Bertie
Umpkin

OO-AAR! OI'VE GOTTER GET THIS 'ERE LOAD O' SUGAR-BEET T'MARKET AFORE LUNCH!
PUFF, PANT!
HUR, HUR! HERE COMES OLD BERTIE! RECKON I'LL 'AVE SOME FUN 'ERE!

YAAAAAAH!
THIS SHOULD GIVE HIM A SHOCK..!
FLOOMPH!
SCREECH!
ERK! SUMMAT'S RUN ACROSS THE ROAD IN FRONT OF OI! MUSTN'T HIT IT... MOIGHT BE A CAT..!

GRAAH! HOW DARE YOU COVER ME IN SUGAR BEET, YOU 'ORRIBLE MAN! GET THIS LOT CLEANED UP SHARP!
HO, HO! NOW FOR SOME MORE LARKS!

AH DEARIE ME... THIS BE A LONG OLE JOB!
MY OFFICIAL TRANSPORT SEEMS TO HAVE SUFFERED SOMEWHAT!
QUIETLY DOES IT..!

WHACK!
WHACK!
YERK, YERK! WHAT A NASTY LAD I AM! NOW, BACK TO COVER!

WHEN BERTIE TRIED TO START HIS TRACTOR...
DANG OI... SUMMAT'S UP WITH MOI TRACTOR..!
HAVIN' TROUBLE, MATE? HUR, HUR!
STRAIN!
QUIVER!
LRRRR!

GAAH! THERE BE A LUMP O' WOOD STUCK IN THE EXHAUST PIPE!
HMMF!
PHH!
HO, HO, HO! WHAT A LAUGH! CHUCKLE!

COOOR!
WHOOOOOSH!
HEE, HEE! THE POOR FOOL! HEH, HEH!
POP!
LURCH!
BRRRRMM!

PROYING!
YELP!
TUM-TEE-TUM!

WAH! I'VE BEEN STUNG!
THUNK!
ZZZOOO-AAAOWW!
ZIP!

SAY! THIS BE A ROIGHT OLE CARRY ON!
GUUUURRRGH!
OOOOMMPPHHH!
SPLOOSH!

ASSAULTING, BATTERING AND SOAKING A COPPER AND HIS TRUSTY BIKE! IT'S DOWN TO THE STATION WITH YOU, ME LAD!
THAT'S WHAT OI LOIKES ABOUT THE COUNTRY-SIDE... ALWAYS SUMMAT HAPPENING..!

Partridge's Patch

BRINDLE AND TOM JOINED THE SEARCH...
THOSE GANGSTERS MAY BE NOWHERE NEAR HERE! BUT WE MUSTN'T LEAVE A STONE UNTURNED, PARTRIDGE! WE'LL ASK SOME QUESTIONS IN THE NEXT VILLAGE...!
THAT'S FUNNY! THAT SMOKE'S COMING FROM WHERE OLD JIM'S COTTAGE IS. NEVER KNOWED HIM LIGHT A FIRE BEFORE!

TOM TURNED INTO THE FOREST...
THIS IS NO TIME TO VISIT YOUR COUNTRY PALS, PARTRIDGE!
JIM'S COTTAGE'D BE AS GOOD A HIDIN' PLACE AS ANY, INSPECTOR. AND... LOOK UP THERE! SOMETHING... OR SOMEONE'S SENT THE BIRDS SCURRYIN' UP INTO THE AIR!

OLD JIM WAS NOT ALONE...
MIND IF WE COME IN, JIM? MAYBE YOU CAN HELP US!
WELL... ALL RIGHT! OH, THIS... THIS IS MY... MY NEPHEW! BEEN STAYIN' WITH ME THE PAST WEEK!

WE AIN'T SEEN NOBODY, INSPECTOR. ME AND MY UNCLE HAVE BEEN ON OUR OWN HERE ALL WEEK!
THAT'S STRANGE!

TOM HAD ALREADY SEEN SOMETHING THAT AROUSED HIS CURIOSITY...
YOU WON'T MIND IF I LOOK AROUND A BIT, WILL YOU, JIM?
FOR PETE'S SAKE! WHAT FOR?

THERE... THERE'S NO ONE ELSE HERE, TOM. AND DON'T BOTHER TO LOOK IN THAT SHED. NOBODY'S BEEN INSIDE IT FOR MONTHS...!

TOM LOOKED AROUND HIM... AND KNEW THAT HIS SUSPICIONS WERE RIGHT...
YOU HEARD MY UNCLE! THERE'S NOBODY HERE BUT US!
EXCEPT A MAN WITH A GUN! AND I KNOW WHERE HE IS!
HAVE YOU SPOTTED THE CLUE?

TOM GAVE NO SIGN OF HIS THOUGHTS...
SORRY TO HAVE BOTHERED YOU THEN! WE'LL BE OFF NOW!
POLICE
AND I SHOULD THINK SO, TOO! LET'S GET OUT OF THIS FOREST!

BUT, INSTEAD, TOM PUT THE POLICE CAR INTO REVERSE, WITH HIS FOOT HARD DOWN ON THE ACCELERATOR. . .
YAAAAAA! PARTRIDGE!... WHAT ARE YOU DOING?
UUUHHHHH!
VROOOM!
CRAAASH!

SLAMMING ON HIS BRAKES, TOM LEAPT INTO ACTION. . .
WHA... WHAT...? MY HEAD...!
GRAB THE BEARDED ONE, INSPECTOR! I'LL BET A YEAR'S PAY ON IT... HE'S NICK CARTER!

TOM WAS RIGHT. . .
GUUUHHHH!
IT IS CARTER! WEARING A FALSE BEARD!
YOU CAME JUST IN TIME! OTHERS ARE COMING. THEY MADE ME LIGHT A FIRE... TO SEND UP A SMOKE SIGNAL!

TEN MINUTES LATER. . .
THEY COULD BE HERE ANY MINUTE!
I CAN'T SEE THEM COMING IN A CAR. . . BECAUSE OF THE ROAD BLOCKS EVERYWHERE! INSPECTOR, I THINK I'VE GOT IT...!

THEY HADN'T TO WAIT LONG. . .
THAT MUST BE THE PLACE! THAT CLEARING WITH THE COTTAGE.
YOU WERE RIGHT AGAIN, PARTRIDGE. THEY'RE GOING TO FLY CARTER AWAY... IN THAT HELICOPTER!

AS THE HELICOPTER TOUCHED DOWN. . .
NICK! NICK! WHERE ARE YOU?
THEY'RE BOTH ARMED, JUST AS I THOUGHT THEY'D BE! SO HERE GOES...!

AS TOM PULLED ON A LENGTH OF STRING...
HUHHH? WHAT... WHAT WAS THAT?
BEES! IT'S A FLIPPIN' BEEHIVE!

NEXT MOMENT...
AAAAHHHHH!
YIIIIIAAAAHHHH!
ZZZZZZZZZZZ
THEY'VE DROPPED THEIR GUNS! WE CAN MOVE IN NOW, INSPECTOR!

UNLIKE THE YELLING CROOKS, TOM AND BRINDLE WERE PROTECTED FROM THE IRATE BEES...
GET US AWAY FROM 'EM!
WE'LL DO THAT! YOU WON'T FIND NO BEES IN JAIL!

WE CAN TAKE THIS GEAR OFF NOW, INSPECTOR. OLD JIM'S CALLING THEM BEES BACK HOME. AIN'T IT WONDERFUL THE WAY EVEN BEES KNOW A FRIEND? THEY WON'T STING HIM!
WE'VE GOT 'EM ALL! BUT, PARTRIDGE...HOW DID YOU KNOW?

FIRST, TOM LED THE INSPECTOR BACK INTO THE COTTAGE...
THAT THERE WERE MIGHTY PECULIAR! THOSE TWO WERE SUPPOSED TO BE ALONE. BOTH OF THEM... TIM AND THE CHAP WHO SAID HE WAS HIS NEPHEW... HAD BEARDS... YET SOMEONE HAD BEEN SHAVING WHEN WE ARRIVED...!
I GET IT! SO IT MEANT THERE WERE EITHER THREE MEN HERE... OR THE BEARD WAS A FALSE ONE. BUT WHAT ABOUT THE GUNMAN... HOW DID YOU KNOW HE WAS IN THAT SHED?

OUTSIDE...
OLD JIM GAVE ME THE CLUE. HE MADE A POINT OF SAYING NO ONE HAD BEEN IN THIS SHED FOR MONTHS! YET YOU CAN SEE WHERE THE WEEDS AND BUSHES HAVE BEEN BROKEN DOWN... BY SOMEONE PULLING OPEN THE DOOR!

ISN'T IT LUCKY OLD JIM HADN'T THE HEART TO CUT DOWN ALL THIS UNDERGROWTH? WE WOULDN'T HAVE HAD A CLUE OTHERWISE! FUNNY HOW NATURE ALWAYS SEEMS TO HELP OUT US POLICEMEN, ISN'T IT?
THE END.

"LADIES and gentlemen, you are about to witness that prince of policemen, Superintendent Smarmy of Scotland Yard, in his hour of triumph, as he at last claps handcuffs on his arch-enemy, Public Enemy Number One, the king of crime himself!

"Stand by to see . . . *the arrest of the Dwarf!*"

A hubbub of excitement broke out in the big hall, crammed with goggling people. The great moment had been carefully staged. All eyes were on the velvet curtain which hid the platform at the side of the hall, and the clacking tongues were suddenly stilled in an expectant hush.

The curtain swept aside.

There on the stage was Superintendent Smarmy, a masterful figure in his resplendent uniform, his handsome face composed in a grim and arrogant smile. From his left hand dangled a pair of handcuffs, and his right hand was poised on high.

The hand was about to fall on the shoulder of the Dwarf.

The master-criminal was in the act of running away from his pursuer, but it was obvious that he could not escape. A tiny man, only four feet tall, he was clad in a skin-hugging costume of black, and his sleek black hair moulded his skull like a cap.

He was looking back over his shoulder at the Super, a snarl of fury distorting his face as he saw the hand of the law descending to trap him, and thus end his unparalleled career of crime.

The crowd in the hall roared with glee. This was the moment the world had been waiting for. The fantastic arch-criminal who had carried out a staggering succession of singlehanded coups and amassed a million pounds in loot, and whom Superintendent Smarmy had been powerless to check, was at last to pay the penalty for his crimes.

The dramatic moment of his arrest could be savoured to the full, as well. Because it was two full minutes since the curtains had parted to reveal Superintendent Smarmy and the Dwarf on the stage, and they were still in the same attitudes now!

In fact, the scene on the stage was a tableau. The hall was inside a London waxworks museum. And the figures of Superintendent Smarmy and the Dwarf were dummies!

Superintendent Smarmy himself was sitting in the front row of the crowded hall. He had been invited to this public unveiling of the museum's latest attraction and was showing gracious approval of his own waxwork likeness.

"You've made my nose a trifle on the modest side, perhaps," he told the museum director, displaying his handsome profile to the crowd behind him. "The features are not quite *noble* enough, do you think? The jaw could be a shade more *commanding*, and perhaps you've done less than justice to my exceptionally manly good looks, but the general effect is not bad, not bad at all."

"You like the action you're shown performing, eh, Super?" the museum director asked with a smile.

"Ahem, yes. Most suitable," answered Smarmy, but a shadow passed over his face.

"Well, of course I know you haven't yet *actually* arrested the Dwarf," the museum director said hastily, "but you undoubtedly will very soon, and there seemed no harm in our anticipating your triumph."

"Quite, quite," said Smarmy, smiling again. "The Dwarf has had the luck of the devil so far, curse him, but he won't dare to defy me much longer."

The words were hardly out of his mouth when a women screamed at the back of the hall.

A hush fell on the crowd, and in the silence a man shouted: "Look! That waxwork dummy of the Dwarf! It's . . . *moving!*"

It was true. The figure of the arch-villain was drawing itself up on the stage and striking an attitude of brazen defiance. The legs flexed and the arms flourished. The sleek black head turned to face the crowd.

A wicked grin creased the devilish face of the figure.

"It's not a waxwork dummy at all!" shouted another man. *"It's the Dwarf himself!"*

"Oh n-no!" stammered Superintendent Smarmy.

"Oh yes!" crowed the Dwarf.

The master-criminal bowed mockingly to his stunned audience and then turned to the waxwork dummy of the Scotland Yard man.

He took the handcuffs out of the dummy's hand and raised the left arm to join the upraised right arm. He snapped the handcuffs around both wax wrists. Then he stepped back, leapt with fantastic agility into the air, and delivered a two-footed kick at the dignified effigy of his arch-enemy.

The dummy Superintendent Smarmy fell flat on its back and lay there, handcuffed, helpless and ridiculous, a figure of fun.

"Ladies and gentlemen," cried the Dwarf, in a malicious imitation of the announcement earlier, "you have just witnessed the humiliation of that poltroon of a policeman, Superintendent Smarmy of Scotland Yard, at the hands of the genius he will never catch, the monarch of mayhem, the emperor of impudence, the overlord of the underworld. . . . myself!

"And just to rub it in, the Dwarf will now carry out another of his audacious crimes, in front of your very eyes!"

Elastic getaway!

Superintendent Smarmy snarled with rage and hurled himself at the platform.

"Grab the little demon, you fools!" he yelled to the policemen who were gaping from among the crowd.

The Dwarf chuckled, stooped, and eased off the safety catches built into the heels of his shoes.

As Smarmy clambered on to the platform and made a furious lunge at him, the arch-criminal stamped hard on the wooden floorboards.

Powerful steel springs uncoiled from inside his heels. With a nonchalant wave to the Superintendent, who was left grasping air, the Dwarf was hurled upwards by his amazing spring-heels and catapulted clean over the heads of the gaping crowd towards the far side of the hall.

Sixty feet from the platform, the Dwarf landed with fantastic dexterity on the narrow ledge of a window which overlooked the street.

The window was open. He stepped over the sill to the ledge which ran along the facade of the waxworks museum.

The crowd in the hall fought their way out of the exits and surged into the street to join the people already gathering there. Superintendent Smarmy was somewhere in the throng, red-faced, baffled, and looking a lot less masterful than the dummy which his enemy had treated so disrespectfully.

The Dwarf was climbing up the front of the build-

With his fantastic spring-heeled boots, the Dwarf was able to hurtle above the heads of the amazed crowd . . .

ing to the huge banner which stretched across the facade and announced: THE DWARF AND SUPERINTENDENT SMARMY ON SHOW ALL THIS WEEK!

Perched on a ledge under the banner, and taking a pressurised spray gun from a clip on his belt, the Dwarf made some lightning alterations to the lettering. When he had finished, the crowd in the street gasped and then guffawed.

The banner now read: THE DWARF PUTS SUPERINTENDENT SMARMY RIGHT UP THE CREEK!

The arch-criminal turned and acknowledged the roar of the crowd with an airy wave of his arm. Then he unclipped another strange appliance from his belt.

This was a self-powered grapnel gun, with a coil of super-fine and specially-treated rope attached to it. The Dwarf was an inventor of genius, and made all his own equipment in the workshop of his secret hideout in the London suburbs.

By the time the Dwarf turned to face the street again, a file of policemen were shuffling along the ledge towards him from either side.

The Dwarf waited until the policemen were a few feet from him, and reaching out with their clumsy hands. Then he lifted the grapnel gun, aimed it towards the building across the gulf of the street, and fired.

The three-pronged grapnel rocketed over the thirty yard gap and hooked itself on a high ledge of the building opposite. The rope stretched from the grapnel to the Dwarf's hands, and he swiftly made it fast to a projection on the wall behind him.

Then, as the crowd in the street below sucked breath into a thousand throats in a gasp of amazement, the master-criminal stepped coolly on to the gossamer-fine rope and began to walk across it.

The Dwarf did not rely only on his mechanical genius to carry out his amazing crimes. Though he was half as tall as the average man, his tiny body was perfectly proportioned, powerfully muscled and incredibly agile.

He walked across the tightrope now with cool balance and control, as easily as though he were walking on a pavement. The goggling crowd surged and eddied fifty feet below, knowing that a single false step would mean death to the tiny figure they were watching.

The policemen on the ledge behind him were just as spellbound. It was Superintendent Smarmy who recalled them to their duty, as he clambered out of a window near the spot where the Dwarf's rope was fastened.

"What are you waiting for, fools?" Smarmy grated. "Can't you see what kind of a building it is across the street? A *jewellery* store! Are you going to let the little villain steal a fortune without trying to stop him?"

The nearest policeman looked down at his size twelve boots.

"What d'you expect us to do, Super?" he muttered. "Walk along that rope after him?"

"Dunderhead!" snapped Smarmy. "What can you do with a rope besides walk on it? I'll tell you. *Cut* it!"

He teetered gingerly along the ledge to where the rope was fastened to the projection. Then he fumbled in his pocket and fished out a big clasp knife.

The Dwarf was more than halfway across now, but he was still ten yards from the safety of the ledge on the building opposite. He checked his delicate stride for a moment, balanced motionless on the taut rope, and looked back.

Superintendent Smarmy was crouching at the end of the rope, the blade of his knife poised over it. He shook with vengeful laughter.

"Stand by for a big let-down, Dwarf!" he bellowed. "You're pretty good at walking on a tightrope, but now try walking on air!"

The crowd massed in the street below gave a gasp of horror. The Dwarf's eyes narrowed. He flexed his knees as though preparing to jump, but it was obvious that even he, with his fantastic athletic powers, could not reach safety from where he was standing.

Balanced on the flimsy rope, fifty feet above the gulf of the street, the Dwarf faced certain death, with a mocking smile on his lips.

Superintendent Smarmy slashed his knife across the rope with a snarl of triumph, and severed it. The crowed groaned.

But this was no ordinary rope. It had been fabricated in the mysterious workshop of the Dwarf. Now, instead of falling limply from the knife, it snapped

As the elastic rope was cut, the Dwarf grabbed one end . . . and was whisked towards the building on the opposite side of the road!

away through the air like elastic under tension.

TWAAAAANG!

The Dwarf had stooped and grasped the rope with his hands as the Super cut it. Now the elasticated rope was recoiling towards the building opposite, and carrying the Dwarf with it. Instead of falling, the master-criminal was being catapulted through the air towards the ledge on the building opposite.

The Scotland Yard man howled with frustration. The crowd gasped. The Dwarf landed on the ledge with both feet, steadied himself, and turned nonchalantly to face the street.

He bowed to the thousand upturned faces of the crowd. He grinned with devilish impudence at the glowering Smarmy. He waved an airy hand.

"Once more, the king of crime cheats death!" he cried. "And now to reward myself for my incredible skill and bravery! Inside the building I am standing on is a fortune in jewellery! It shall soon glitter and glisten with the rest of my loot, in the fabulous hoard of the Dwarf!"

Vacuum cleaner raid

The secret of the Dwarf's success was the care with which he prepared his fantastic crimes.

On the facade of the jewellery store, three floors above the street and facing the waxworks museum opposite, was a giant sign bearing the name of the store and the royal coat of arms.

Behind this sign, the night before his dramatic appearance in the waxworks museum, the Dwarf had concealed a certain object which he had already stolen from a place nearby.

After bowing to the crowd below, the Dwarf stepped out of sight behind the sign. He picked up the hidden object, checked that it was all in order, and threw it out along the ledge in full view of the crowd.

The Dwarf himself remained hidden behind the sign. He heard the crowd yell with amazement as they spotted the object he had thrown out. As he had anticipated, the sight of it was causing a sensation.

With a crafty grin on his face, the Dwarf turned to the window behind him. Still hidden by the sign, he unclipped a razor-sharp cutting tool from his belt. Five seconds' work removed the glass from the window. He peered through the frame.

He was looking into the main showroom of the jewellery store. In display cases all round the big room, diamonds sparkled and glittered.

The shop assistants, and the policemen who had joined them in the store at the first threat of the Dwarf's nefarious intentions, were all clustered at the windows of the room.

As the Dwarf had guessed they would, when he planned this crime, the men who should have been guarding the precious jewellery were absorbed in watching the object which he had taken from its concealment behind the sign a moment before, and tossed out on to the ledge.

The Dwarf chuckled silently, listening to the excited hubbub of the crowd in the street below, the clanging of fire engines, the wailing of police car sirens, and the bellowing roar which was Superintendent Smarmy making himself heard above the din.

"My decoy plan has worked," the Dwarf murmured to himself. "Now I can collect my loot, at leisure and undisturbed."

He climbed nimbly through the empty frame of the window. Unclipping from his belt a small nozzle-shaped instrument attached by a fat rubber tube to a satchel strapped to his side, he strolled unhurriedly towards the display cases.

None of the shop assistants or policemen noticed him. Their eyes were glued to the window panes. And the Dwarf was moving as silently as a shadow.

The arch-criminal opened the first display case with a power-operated picklock, aimed the nozzle-shaped instrument at the loaded shelves inside, and switched it on.

The instrument was a miniature but fantastically powerful vacuum cleaner. Within ten seconds, it had sucked up all the diamond brooches and pearl necklaces in the display case and transferred them under forced draught via the rubber tube to the Dwarf's satchel.

The shop assistants and policemen at the windows of the showroom had heard nothing. The noise in the street outside drowned the faint hum of the mechanical loot-collector which the grinning Dwarf was using behind their backs.

The master-criminal strolled unhurriedly from display case to display case, transferring their priceless contents to his satchel. When he had completed his circuit of the room, and collected every jewel on view, he turned his attention to a huge steel safe which stood in a corner.

The safe was made of steel, several inches thick, and its door was studded with dials and knobs of a thief-proof combination lock.

But the Dwarf was no ordinary thief. And he had no intention of bothering with the lock. From his belt he unclipped a weird-looking glove, its leather fingers padded and seamed with metal wires.

The arch-criminal put his right hand into the glove and placed his palm flat against the steel door of the safe. Then he flexed his gloved fingers.

KRRRRRUNCH!

The solid steel of the door dented and dimpled as though it had been made of putty. The Dwarf's gloved fingers just dug into the door, and with a sudden wrench he tore out a whole handful of steel and left a gaping hole in the safe, six inches wide!

The glove was an invention of the Dwarf's. Powered by built-in servo-nuclear energy, it exerted the staggering strength of a hundred bulldozers in each of its fingers. The Dwarf called it his "crusher glove".

It had only one drawback. It was noisy. The Dwarf was reaching into the safe through the hole he had made, and extracting a leather bag containing £50,000 worth of uncut diamonds from inside, when the shop assistants and policemen clustered by the windows on the far side of the room reacted to the

Another one of the Dwarf's amazing inventions—a razor-sharp cutting tool that could slice its way through a plate-glass window . . .

noise of the tearing steel, swung round, and spotted him.

They were thunderstruck. Their mouths dropped open and their eyes saucered. They were still goggling when the Dwarf dropped the last bagful of diamonds into his bulging satchel, grinned at them wickedly, and ran across the showroom to the window he had entered by earlier.

"B-but how d-did the little d-devil d-do it?" gasped one of the shop assistants.

"Don't ask me," breathed a policeman. "I know the Dwarf's a genius, but even he can't be in two places at one and the same time!"

"Listen!" interrupted another shop assistant. "He's explaining the trick to the crowd!"

Above the law!

The Dwarf was standing on the high ledge of the jewellery store overlooking the street. He was holding up his satchel full of loot for the crowd to see, and cackling with devilish laughter.

"My master-plan was designed to draw your attention away from the showroom where the jewellery was displayed!" he cried. "My problem was to think of some object which could rival the breathtaking fascination of myself, and attract all eyes to it while I was stealing the jewellery undisturbed!

"It seemed an insoluble problem, until . . . I remembered the waxworks museum! And suddenly I saw the solution!

"Only one thing in the world could force you to take your admiring gaze away from the Dwarf, and that was . . . *another Dwarf!*"

The Dwarf gestured towards the huge sign behind which he had hidden earlier, and the ledge beyond. From the ledge dangled the object he had taken from its concealment and thrown out into the full view of the crowd.

The object was a lifesize waxwork effigy of himself! It was the dummy whose place he had taken in the museum tableau.

By attaching wires to the dummy Dwarf, the arch-criminal had ensured that when he threw it out from behind the sign, it would fall over the ledge and remain hanging there by its fingertips.

The crowd in the street, and the shop assistants and policemen inside the jewellery store, had imagined that they were looking at the real Dwarf, dangling helpless and unable to move high in the air.

And while they were goggling at his waxwork effigy, and Superintendent Smarmy was mounting a fireman's ladder to lay triumphant hands on his arch-enemy, the Dwarf himself was coolly carrying out his crime inside the jewellery store!

Superintendent Smarmy was still marooned on the fireman's ladder now, within arm's length of the dummy Dwarf hanging from the ledge. The Super's mouth was opening and closing in breathless fury and frustration as the swelling laughter of the crowd rose up to him from the street below.

The Dwarf chuckled victoriously and pressed a button on his belt. Enormous bat-like wings of aluminium and nylon unfolded from the jet-powered pack on his back.

Before he flew away with his loot over the heads of the crowd and the rooftops of London to his secret hideout in the suburbs, the master-criminal had the last word.

"Take back the effigy of myself to the waxworks museum from which I stole it last night," he crowed, looking down at Superintendent Smarmy. "But tell them to display it on its own in future! No paltry policeman's hand will ever fall on the shoulder of the Dwarf. He will never be outwitted! Let the multitude see his effigy in the waxwork museum as they see me here now . . . the Dwarf triumphant, alone and incomparable . . . *above the law!*"

Everyone had been looking at the dummy figure of the Dwarf, clinging by its fingertips to the high ledge . . . while the *real* Dwarf had been engaged on his fabulous jewel raid!

CRAZY CAR CAPERS

ZIS IS OUR *SKIBULLTANK* COMMANDED BY OUR BRAVE COLONEL KUTCH!
MM! IT DOESN'T LOOK VERY FAST, BUT I DON'T LIKE THE LOOK OF KUTCH. I THINK WE'LL HAVE TO WATCH HIM *VERY CAREFULLY!*

THE MUNDAVIANS WASTED NO TIME...
YOU VILL FIND TRACK IS MARKED WITH FLAGS. IT IS RACE ROUND THREE MOUNTAINS AND FINISH BACK HERE. ARE YOU READY?
AYE! IT'LL BE A HA-R-RD RACE BUT MA BONNY *SPORRAN'S* USED TO THE HILLS!
INDEED TO GOODNESS THEY MAKE SNOWDON LOOK LIKE A MOLEHILL!

AS SOON AS THE RACE STARTED, THE FOUR BRITISH CARS LEAPT INTO THE LEAD. BULLDOG HAD BEEN RIGHT. THE SKIBULLTANK WAS INDEED SLOW...
HEH! HEH! THEY DRIVE LIKE MADMEN— BUT MY TURN WILL COME!
OCH! THIS IS GOING TO BE EASIER THAN I THOUGHT!
Rosie

SOME DISTANCE AHEAD, KUTCH'S MEN WERE WAITING...
HERE THEY COME! BE READY TO KNOCK AWAY THE PROPS WHEN I TELL YOU!
AND THEN AVALANCHE WILL *BURY* BRITISHERS!

BUT...
CLUNK!
NOW!
SORRY I CAN'T WAIT, OLD CHAP. I'VE GOT A DATE WITH A WINNING POST!
COME ON, YE MUCKLE-HEADED MONSTER. DINNA STOP NOW! WE'RE IN THE LEAD!

THEY SOON LEARNED WHY KUTCH WAS AMUSED...
GOODBYE, BRITISH TORTOISES! FOR YOU THE RACE IS FINISHED!
LOOK! HE'S USING THE BULLDOZER TO CLEAR A PATH! WE SHALL BE ABLE TO FOLLOW BEHIND HIM!

BUT KUTCH HAD ANOTHER TRICK UP HIS SLEEVE...
HEH! HEH! HEH! MY SKIBULLTANK IS CLEVER MACHINE, YES?
BEJABERS! IT'S RAINING ROCKS! IF THAT SPALPEEN HITS SHAMROCK I'LL MURDER HIM!
SOME MINUTES LATER...
BEGORRAH! ALL THAT STUFF HE THREW BEHIND HIM HAS BLOCKED THE PATH AGAIN. WE'LL NEVER CLEAR IT IN TIME TO CATCH THE ROGUE!
YES, WE WILL! LOOK! THE HEAT FROM ROSIE'S BOILER IS MELTING THE SNOW! IF I GET UP MORE STEAM WE'LL SOON BE ON OUR WAY AGAIN!

AND SO...
CURSES! THEY HAVE GOT THROUGH!
QUICK! WE MUST WARN COLONEL KUTCH!
WE WILL TAKE THIS SHORT CUT AND CATCH UP WITH THE SKIBULLTANK!
THEN THE COLONEL WILL PUT PLAN NUMBER TWO INTO OPERATION!
WHILE THE TWO THUGS SPED ACROSS THE HILLS TO WARN THEIR LEADER, PADDY WAS IN HOT PURSUIT...
SO HE'D THROW ROCKS ON ME OLD SHAMROCK, WOULD HE? I'LL TIE HIM TO ONE O' ME ROCKETS AND LAUNCH HIM INTO SPACE!

THERE HE GOES, THE BLITHERIN' BANSHEE! HE'LL SOON BE TASTING A LUMP OF IRISH FIST!

BUT KUTCH HAD BEEN WARNED...
HERE COMES THE IRISHER! NOW I PRESS THIS BUTTON AND GIVE HIM BIG SURPRISE!

MY SNOW-SHIFTER DEVICE WILL MAKE BRITISHER THINK HE IS IN SNOW-STORM!

KUTCH WAS RIGHT!
BEDAD AND BEGOB! A BLIZZARD! WHERE DID THAT COME FROM?

THAT'S GOT RID OF ONE OF THEM! HO! HO!
'TWAS A DIVILISH TRICK... AN' I FELL FOR IT! AAGH!

WISHT! ME LOVELY SHAMROCK'S BOUNCING LIKE A BALL! IF SHE CAN FIND A SOFT LANDING I'LL BE ALL RIGHT!

PADDY'S WISH WAS GRANTED...
YE LILY-LIVERED SKUNKS! WAIT TILL I GET AT YE!
BAH! HE'LL WARN THE OTHERS! COME ON! LET'S GET AWAY FROM HERE!

WHEN BULLDOG AND ROSIE ARRIVED, PADDY EXPLAINED WHAT HAD HAPPENED...
IT'S CLEAR KUTCH AND HIS THUGS WILL STOP AT NOTHING TO WIN, PADDY, MY OLD PAL! JOIN ME, WE'LL RESCUE SHAMROCK LATER!
YOU'RE RIGHT, BULLDOG. IT BREAKS ME HEART TO LEAVE HER BUT THE FIRST THING TO DO IS TO HELP YOU WIN THIS RACE!
SEE, BOYOS! DIDN'T I TELL YOU TO GET YOURSELVES A LUCKY LEEK? HA! HA!
HEY, DAI! WAIT!
IT'S NO GOOD, BULL-DOG. HE HASN'T HEARD YOU!

♫ WHEN YOU COME HOME AGAIN TO WALES...
OH-HO! A LITTLE TREE ACROSS THE TRACK. I'LL SOON MOVE THAT! ♫

NOW I'LL SOON CATCH UP WITH THAT KUTCH BOYO!
TIME FOR SLEEP, HATED BRITISHER!

OOF!
WELL DONE. NOW TO FINISH JOB PROPERLY..

WHAT DO WE DO WITH HIM?
LEAVE HIM. HIS MACHINE NO GOOD NOW. HE WILL NOT BEAT OUR GLORIOUS KUTCH!

WHEN DAI RECOVERED...
OUCH! WHAT HIT ME?
I DINNA KEN, BUT THIS ELASTIC DIDN'T GET CUT ACCIDENTALLY! DAFFODIL'S OUT O' THE RACE, LADDIE. YE'LL HAVE TO SQUEEZE IN BESIDE ME IN SPORRAN, AND WE'LL GET AFTER 'EM!

SEETHING WITH ANGER, THEY SET OFF IN PURSUIT... AND STRAIGHT INTO KUTCH'S NEXT TRAP!
WHAT THE..?
LOOK, MAC! OVER THERE IN THE TREES, LOOK YOU! KUTCH'S THUGS! LET'S GET THEM!
AFTER THEM, BOYO!
UP THE MACINTOSHES!
WHICH WAS EXACTLY WHAT KUTCH HAD PLANNED!
HEH! HEH! WHILE THEY ARE AWAY ON A WILD GEESES CHASE I WILL POUR THIS SPECIAL MUNDAVIAN ACID INTO THE SCOTTISCHER'S OIL CAN!
A LITTLE LATER...
IT'S A PITY WE DIDN'T CATCH THEM, BOYO! BUT AT LEAST WE STOPPED THEM ATTACKING SPORRAN!
AYE! I'LL JUST GIVE HER A WEE DRAM OF OIL, WHILE YE CLEAR AWAY THE NET!
BLISTERING BAG-PIPES! SPORRAN'S ON FIRE!
FZZZZZZZTT!
WHAT HAPPENED, MAC?
I DINNA KEN AT A'... I JUST POURED OIL INTO THE WORKS AN'... AN'... WELL, YE CAN SEE FOR YOURSELF!
OIL, D'YE SAY? THAT'S NOT OIL! IT'S SOME SORT OF ACID! LOOK!
WE'VE BEEN TRICKED! THAT'S WHY THEY LED US AWAY FROM SPORRAN! OOH! LET ME AT 'EM! STEAM UP, BULLDOG! I'LL MASSACRE THE LOT OF 'EM!

WITH ALL FOUR ABOARD AND WITH ROSIE GOING FLAT OUT, THEY GRADUALLY OVER-HAULED THE SKIBULLTANK!
I'LL JUST POLISH UP ME FIST READY FOR KUTCH'S BIG NOSE!
Rosie
A FEW MORE YARDS, MY FRIENDS, AND WE GIVE THEM ANOTHER SURPRISE, EH?
AS THE SKIBULLTANK REACHED THE BROW OF THE HILL, KUTCH PRESSED ANOTHER BUTTON...
READY, CHAPS..
CLICK
BEDAD! HIS MACHINE'S FITTED WITH SKIS! LOOK!
THEY REACHED THE PEAK AND LOOKED DOWN INTO THE VALLEY BELOW...
WILL YE LOOK AT THAT THING GO! AS IF 'TWERE JET-PROPELLED! WE'LL NEVER CATCH 'EM NOW!
WE'LL KEEP TRYING! LET'S GO!
BUT AS THEY WATCHED...
THEY'VE STOPPED. ONE MAN IS SKI-ING AWAY FROM THE SKIBULLTANK... HI, WHAT ARE YOU DOING, MAC?
I'M GUESSING THAT THEY'RE PLANNING MORE MISCHIEF AND I'M GOING TO FOLLOW THAT VILLAIN. I'LL BORROW ROSIE'S BUMPERS, MON!
Rosie
GO ON, BOYO! HE'S USED TO THE SNOW IN SCOTLAND, SEE?
THESE MAD HIGHLANDERS HAVE THEIR USES AFTER ALL. GOOD LUCK, MAC!
AS HE PREPARED THE FINAL TRAP, KUTCH'S ASSISTANT HAD NO IDEA THAT HE HAD BEEN FOLLOWED...
HE'S MOVING THE FLAGS SO THAT THEY LEAD TO THE DANGEROUS BRIDGE! THEN I BET HE'LL HIDE THE SIGN. KUTCH WILL DRIVE OVER THE UNMARKED BRIDGE, AND WHEN BULLDOG COMES HE'LL FOLLOW THE FLAGS TO THE UNSAFE BRIDGE!
DANGER! KEEP OFF! BRIDGE UNSAFE
MAC WAS RIGHT, BUT AS THE MUNDAVIAN STARTED TO COVER THE DANGER SIGN...
DANGER
HEY, MISTER...